Room for Happiness

by
Erik van Praag

English Translation by Anne Scheinberg

AmErica House
Baltimore

© 2001 by Erik van Praag.
All rights reserved. No part of this book may be reproduced in any form without written permission from the publishers, except by a reviewer who may quote brief passages in a review to be printed in a newspaper or magazine.

First printing

ISBN: 1-58851-913-9
PUBLISHED BY AMERICA HOUSE BOOK PUBLISHERS
www.publishamerica.com
Baltimore

Printed in the United States of America

Prologue

An unexamined life is not worth living.
– Socrates

My life has actually been a very ordinary one. I come from a complete family: father, mother, two boys, two girls. No divorces or terrifying diseases. Death has not played any exceptional role in my life—at least not during my youth.

My father was a teacher. My mother stayed home. We weren't rich, but we seemed to have enough for what we needed. We lived in a beautiful house on the river.

I was generally happy at school. I loved to read and make music. At first I believed in Santa Claus; later I didn't. I never believed in the stork or the tooth fairy. We were humanists; we lived free of the pressure of church or village life.

I grew and thrived, like my brothers and sisters. I studied, married, had children and a job, followed a career, got sick and then got better...yes, my life has been, up to now, an ordinary one.

The way I felt about life was quite changeable. I was frequently happy and satisfied, but frequently neither. In those moments I was restless, or had a vague sense of unease. There was actually no reason for this, since I had—and have—everything my heart desired and for which I had worked: a nice house, prosperity, a dear family, satisfying work, friends. There were, nevertheless, moments in my life when I felt so awful that I sought professional help. I went into psychotherapy.

This therapy—finally, after much time, effort, and money—provided what I had hoped for: happiness, inner peace (at least most of the time) and a new sense of perspective. The therapy also allowed me to appreciate and enjoy what there was: my wife and children, holidays, work, sex, in fact, everything. I no longer needed to destroy the things I had built up. You see, I had always had the tendency—against my deeper desires—to corrupt what I had. Through depression, unreasonable aggression, or dictatorial behavior, I could always manage to take situations that were actually really pleasant and turn them into extremely unpleasant conflicts and dramas. Now that is past...well, there is more to tell about it, but that comes later.

Therapy is actually nothing else than self-examination. It is learning to look at yourself without judgement. Even before I started therapy, I had made a commitment to this. Somewhere around the end of my teens, or perhaps even long before—with support, perhaps, from my guardian angel, who knows? but again: more about that later—I had made two fundamental decisions. The first was: I won't live a mediocre life. It is not that I have to be rich or famous—even though that might be nice. It is rather that I want to have excellence and quality in my life. When it is all over, I want to be able to say: this was the best life that I could possibly live.

The second decision was: I will be honest towards myself. I won't delude myself; I won't lead myself up the garden path. I will even, if necessary, look at myself with brutal honesty. Not to punish or condemn, but also not to conceal what there is to see.

Don't ask me *why* I made these decisions. I don't know. I can't even remember exactly either when or how I came to decide them. I only know that at a certain time, they were part of me. Later, in dark or aggressive moments, I sometimes forgot. But they always came back. And as a result of the therapy, they were strengthened. Since then, I have never forgotten them for long.

Room for Happiness

For a long time, I didn't believe that these decisions were anything special. And in one sense they are not: anyone can make them. But I have noticed that there are a great many people who do not make them, or who don't make them in this manner. And I have also noticed that they have major consequences for how your life develops. Or rather: they are critical to how you *experience* your life. Because once you, like me, make these decisions, your life appears richer, more adventurous, and more satisfying. You might even say happier. In this sense, happiness is there for the taking. There is always space for happiness and good fortune. You also live in a different relationship with fear, in the sense that it no longer determines your life.

It is actually not the case that if you choose to be honest about yourself and to live a non-mediocre life, your life in fact becomes more noticeable. As I said: my life has really been very ordinary. But it is becoming much more exciting. Suddenly you see your life as one coherent adventure. There is a story line, there are developments, it all makes sense. Apparently accidental events, that appear to be without deep import, suddenly take on much greater meaning and have much greater emotional impact. Sadness is deeper, joy greater. Your sense of time changes: there suddenly appears to be much more time. This is a natural result of experiencing so much. At the same time things happen much faster: time flies by. You might recognize this experience as characterizing a time that you have lived with great intensity: when you were in love, or had an unbelievably wonderful vacation, or during a workshop.

I believe that being honest towards yourself and striving beyond the mediocre can produce great things in your life. That is why it has often surprised me that so few people choose this. Now I understand it a bit better. Choosing honesty towards yourself and striving for something beyond the mediocre makes life richer, but not always easier. Feelings become more intense, and this includes the "negative" feelings like sadness and disappointment. (At the same time it seems that if you accept these feelings without resistance, they are not as completely negative as you think. It can also be very liberating to experience pain). In each of us there are thoughts, imaginings, feelings and ambitions which we would actually rather not have. Noone finds it pleasant to scrutinize his own cruelty; to face his fear; or to discover attitudes and values that came from his parents, and which he had thought to have abolished years ago.

That's why many therapists and teachers state that it demands courage to look inside yourself, and to admit what you really want for your life. And that last is also a prerequisite for more than a mediocre life. "The person who has the courage to know himself, is the warrior of the heart," says Danaan Parry. A "warrior of the heart" is someone who helps himself and others to look at themselves. This was a specific function in some traditional Native American tribes, next to the function of chief or shaman. This was the case because the tribes believed that seeing yourself clearly is necessary to be able to benefit yourself and others. The Bible says this too. You can only love your neighbor as much as you love yourself, but to love yourself you must accept yourself, and to do this you have to know what is inside of you.

In summary, self-observation and striving to your highest potential enriches your life. Or to say it another way: you live more consciously. In other words: your life becomes a great adventure in learning. I believe that life is to enjoy, and to grow. You could also say: to learn in and to learn from. And as I said, because I have chosen to look at my life in this way, I find it much more interesting and instructive. Events which at first weren't so interesting, and that I have appreciated only as information, are now meaningful. This results in additional events occurring, which in turn are even more fascinating.

For me this also means that I increasingly use events from my own life as illustrations in my work as educator and management trainer. Initially, I had a certain amount of resistance to this. I was afraid to show my naked self: I feared that I wouldn't be understood, and that I would therefore get hurt. I also didn't want to draw attention to myself. But along the way I began to experiment with this, and I noticed that my listeners were often very interested in my accounts. And this is of course primarily because they recognized things in these stories which resonated in their own lives. Thus these stories contributed to the people around me being able to look more gently towards their own lives, and thus at themselves. And that, in turn, has enriched *their* lives.

This is the reason that I have decided to write some of these stories down, so that they can benefit a greater public. The result is the book that you have before you. Most of the accounts are from my own life, but a couple of them have been told to me by others. Once you begin to give your attention to the stories in your own life, other people begin to give you their stories as well. And then you begin to see that although we each are each playing our own part, together we are all part of a huge concert, a giant piece of music, with the world as concert hall. Will be play in harmony or disharmony? I think that we can choose for ourselves, once we know what we are playing.

Each time I tell my story, I feel a need to give my teacher the floor. Who is my teacher? Sometimes I am. Sometimes it is the knowledge and experience that I have taken in, directly or from books. Sometimes it is my intuition. Or my guardian angel. Or Life Itself. And sometimes it is the understanding and insights of others, people who have actually played or who still play the role of teacher in my daily life.

Sometimes my teacher speaks in my inner voice, sometimes in the voice of another. I consciously became acquainted with my teacher in my youth (see the story High-Diving). I am convinced that there is a teacher available to each person at every moment, but you have to be willing to listen to him or her, or perhaps you don't get the information. In any case my teacher often has wise lessons and referrals about how to manage; that is why, at the end of each story, I give him the floor. He will then illustrate what I can learn from the particular event, and perhaps also what you can learn.

Once I have told all of the stories that I want to tell in this book, there is a closing chapter, where I summarize what my conception of life has become as it has been formed by these experiences. (Note added in 2001: this was in 1994. Some things I would have said slightly differently nowadays). Not because it is the right conception, but so that you can get an idea of how you can come to greater awareness through your own life stories. That includes an invitation for you to do the same with your own life. From my own experience I know that—if some of the stories that I tell touch you somewhere—this will surely occur.

In closing, I would like in this introduction to thank several people. In the first place, my family and friends, my teachers and colleagues, and all the people who play a role in this book. I want to thank them for what they have given me, but also for the fact that they, insofar as I have asked them, had no problem with appearing in this book. And I would like to thank my publisher, Madeleine Klis, for serving as the first critical reader, who urged me to be much clearer about what I have to say.

I wish you much reading pleasure. Or, pleasure reading aloud. Many of us often forget how much extra pleasure reading aloud can provide. For those that only do this at Christmas, there is also a Christmas story in the book: "The Good Shepherd." (And in a certain sense also, *"In Memoriam Patris"*).

Cindy

I don't believe that in our hearts we like to damage or hurt others. Nevertheless certain people appear to be sadistic, or to humiliate others, or only to push others around in their own claimed interest. What is the source of this? To find an answer, I only have to look inside.

I have felt a destructive rage in myself as long as I can remember. I have never tortured or trapped insects; probably the idea never occurred to me. No, it was worse. I tortured and teased children who were weaker than me. And when I was nine I experimented with a little kitten. I threw it as up high as I could into the air, and "enjoyed" the terror of the little animal. The cat (and I) were rescued when a neighbor saw what I had done. She screamed, and both the cat and I ran away.

It was at about this age that I became obsessed with a wish to see someone fall into the water. Whenever I saw a river or a canal, I had all kinds of fantasies of drowning or nearly drowning people (incidentally, I myself almost drowned in the ocean during this period, but that is a different story...or is there some connection?). Finally, I couldn't stand it any longer. One afternoon I was playing with the girl next door, Cindy, on the quay by our house. I seduced her to the edge, and, once we arrived, after what seemed to be an eternity of inner conflict, I pushed her over the edge. Splash! There she went, falling between the sea wall and the ships that were lying there. She couldn't swim.

I was in shock, and ran away. But I—or Cindy—had a guardian angel. A woman on one of the boats had seen it happening, and the last thing that I heard was, "Child overboard!" I fled home, to the attic, unable to think a single thing besides "I did it, I did it." I didn't know if she was drowned or saved. I felt guilty, but amazingly enough, I believe that the shame was stronger.

If I remember right, I waited until the next day to do anything about it. It was Sunday morning, and we were having coffee and cake. I hadn't heard anything further; nothing had happened; noone had called. I couldn't hold out any longer, and I confessed all to my parents. They were floored, and my father went immediately to the neighbors. He came back at once: Cindy appeared to be well and healthy—she had gotten a sniffle, that was all. It turned out that her parents hadn't the slightest idea that I had deliberately pushed her into the water.

And there I sat facing my parents. "For Heaven's sake, why did you do that?" asked my father. If only I knew the answer. They weren't even really angry; they seemed to understand that it fell a bit outside of the normal range of events. After all, I was normally an obedient child.

Nevertheless I had to be punished. The decision was that I had to take my cake to Cindy, and tell her that I was sorry. To the present day I don't know if it was a wise verdict, for a verdict it was! I found it dreadful to do, since I was dying of shame. Oddly enough, on many levels: because we had cake on Sunday, they probably didn't (I believe that they were poorer than we). But also, it made it perfectly clear that I had pushed her on purpose—up till then, it could have appeared to be an accident. I was deeply humiliated (perhaps a new source of cruelty?). But my father was relentless. I believe that neither Cindy nor her parents understood much of what had happened. I was always such a good boy, wasn't I? The event was beyond their capacity to imagine.

Later, during my training as a psychologist, I read many explanations of the possible causes of my aggression and sadism. War experiences; a nice, ultimately reasonable but quite closed and absent father; a mother who let her unconscious aggression and rules limit her love—I had all this and more to contend with. And even my "good boyishness" could well have been a symptom of repressed frustration and aggression. I indeed experienced all of that as well in my therapy. Perhaps it is indeed a partial explanation of the situation, but it is mainly an explanation of why it is that we all have our own hidden feelings and needs.

However, that is not the greatest significance of the experience. It has taught me to understand the destructiveness and sadism of others. It has taught me to distinguish between the behavior of the person—which I can detest—and the person themself, whom I do not want to judge. It has taught me to understand the words of the Bible: "Let him who is without sin be the first to throw a stone." And it taught me gratitude: I was "saved by the bell." You can't even imagine how I would have felt and how my life would have been affected if Cindy had drowned, to say nothing of the effect it could have had on both of our parents. Should we have guardian angels who coach and guide us, and who protect us from unimaginable disasters? Through this experience, and the one that follows in "High Diving," I have come to believe this in my heart of hearts.

Message from my Teacher

In the last paragraph, there is already plenty that has been said. But there is still more to say.

In the first place, this situation illustrates how lives are woven together with each other. We humans are creators, creating our own reality, but we do this in a process of co-creation with each other and with life itself. This event was as important for Cindy as it was for me. There is also a great deal to learn for our respective parents. Each of the involved people can take away their own experiences and lessons for living, and that is one of the reasons why they came into contact with each other in this way, and together wrote this chapter of their lives—at any rate, at that moment in their lives.

In the second place, notice how much energy repressed feelings can have. I sometimes compare the internal power of human beings with the hidden power of the atom, which is released by splitting or fusion. You wouldn't say, on first glance, how much force is hidden within. The same holds for a person. When the power is released, there can be a terrible explosion. This can turn out to be destructive, as in the example above, but it doesn't have to be. That same force can be used to create something good. It lies within us humans to make the choices.

Everyone has a destructive side. This gets shaped in this life, but it is already present at birth. It is actually not important where it comes from. It is important to face this aspect. In one person, it can manifest as destructive rage or violence (as in my case; see also the story "Crisis"); in another it can come out in power struggles, selfishness, failing to take responsibility, disease, etc. That is what traditional Christianity calls "sin."

But in contrast to what is learned through the teachings of predestination, this sin is not a burden with which we are bowed down, and from which we cannot break free. On the contrary, it is even an expression of life force itself, that can be transformed into the healing power of love.

In order to be able to do that, you first have to discover this "sin" in yourself. To face your destructive side—without judging yourself. To feel the pain of it. To learn to look at yourself with compassion. This demands courage and willingness, and also a certain amount of time and discipline to look towards yourself at regular intervals. It can be a while before you begin to see results, but it always works if you really want it to. The further that you come, the more you can mean for the world around you and the better you will feel about yourself.

The Diving Board

Did you dare, as a child, to jump from the high diving board in the swimming pool? Or even to dive? From the "High Whip" as we said in Dordrecht? Well, not me. I was a fine swimmer, but I absolutely didn't dare to dive from the high board. It scared me to death. That wasn't a problem, of course. Until that terrible day (or was it a good one?)...

"Come on, boys, everyone from the high diving board," said the swim coach during school swim (I was ten, perhaps eleven at the time). My heart leapt into my throat. Two terrors struggled with each other: the fear to go up and jump off, and the terror of failing to do so and making a fool of myself in front of the critical eyes of my friends (and the *girls*...). Already, I had a less than heroic reputation, as far as it concerned physical activity, and that was not great for my popularity, or at least, so I believed.

On the ground, the fear of making a fool of myself won out. I was careful not to stand in the beginning of the queue, but my turn finally came. Just that steep, steel ladder was already terrifying. By halfway up my fear had gripped me by the throat. But I reached the top. There I became so panicked that the reactions of my mates didn't matter anymore. To their looks of surprise and the sound of a few snickers I climbed back down. It would have been less noticeable had I simply remained on the ground. I felt thoroughly miserable.

I rode home in a deep funk. I began to rationalize; at that age I was already plenty good at it. I said to myself that leading a successful life or becoming a valuable person of course doesn't depend on whether you can jump from the high diving board. And that if my friends should reject me because I didn't dare, they were not real friends. A "real" friend should accept me for who really I was. All very true...only too bad that these rationalizations didn't help me. A quiet but nevertheless clear voice inside kept saying: "Hey, hey, that's not what it's about, as you well know..." It kept me feeling uncomfortable, and gradually it got through to me that it didn't have to do with the reactions of my friends. In short, I couldn't feel good about myself if I were to leave it like that. I knew, of course, that it wasn't truly dangerous, that it wouldn't really hurt me. My fear was completely irrational.

As far as I can remember, it was not about jacking up my mutilated self-respect. Even at that age I knew that that sort of fear didn't have to do with being "good" or "bad." You can't do much about it in the moment: the fear is simply there. (That makes me think about the story of the Two Generals, but more on that later...). It doesn't make you a bad or stupid person. No, it had to do with something deeper; at that moment I didn't know precisely what. I understood that only much later. At the time I knew only one thing: I had to jump off that board one time, or the bad feelings would stick with me forever. In my childish wisdom I also considered something else: I needed to find a situation where I could do it without being forced, neither by friends or acquaintances who might encourage me or put me down, nor through a public too impatient to wait for me.

I therefore chose a grey day, and asked my mother for a quarter for the (outdoor) swimming pool. "Today? You want to swim today?" she asked in surprise. But when I insisted, she agreed.

The pool was in fact almost completely empty. There was only one lonely woman swimming laps. I went to the deep end and looked at the high diving board. There stood the monster. After a few minutes, it was abundantly clear to me that it must happen. The possibility of returning home with the deed undone was so unbearable that I rejected it. I walked to the diving board and climbed upwards.

It is easy now to write this, but those steps were some of the most heaviest in my life. After all these years I still have great respect for that small boy, who did it in spite of it all. I sometimes believe that this laid the basis not only for my own self-respect, but also for my respect and love for others (from whom I know that everyone is able to take such a step, and also that everyone at least once in their lives gets the opportunity to make it).

In deep panic, but still in control, I walked to the end of the board, looked over the precipice (this must sound ridiculous to anyone who has not known this particular fear) and...jumped! At once, even during the fall, I felt the enormous satisfaction and triumph; the fear disappeared and I landed in the water. Liberation! Hallelujah! The world is mine! Victory! I swam to the side and climbed out of the pool.

There, I turned around and looked at the diving tower. What do you think? I suddenly realized something very shocking: I was still afraid. *But now get through it*, I thought. So I returned to the board, climbed up again, still terrified (but nevertheless beginning to be accustomed to the fear and to get a sense of trust), jumped again, and swam again to the side. I climbed out and looked again at the board. I realized that I was still afraid. And then suddenly the light went on: "Aha! So I am afraid of high diving boards! And that is ok! It doesn't mean that I necessarily have to jump off of them!" Satisfied, I took one more dive (from the side!) and rode home.

It was only many years later that I learned to fully value the significance of this experience. I have already said something about how it strengthened my capacity for self-respect and love for others. I understood that even irrational fear can be absolutely real. Through this experience I also learned that fear doesn't have to stop you. An observation of inestimable value, which was often of great use to me later in my life, and which has proved to be one of the most important things which I, as a therapist and management trainer, was able to—and still can—teach others.

What caused a small boy so creatively to turn such an experience of initial failure into a positive learning experience? I can imagine two answers to this question, and they might both be true. One: we create our own learning experiences, but sometimes at a moment or from a reality (the source where we all ultimately spring from) that is far removed from the ordinary reality of the moment in which the actual situation occurs. Two: we are guided. A guardian angel leads us through the crises in our lives, and helps us to transform a crisis from a merely dangerous situation to one that is full of possibilities. Personally, I believe in both.

But this story isn't yet over. Years later we stayed with the International Saturday Group, a large group of therapists and their clients and families from many different countries, in a summer camp on Madeira, with the goal of working on our personal growth in an atmosphere conducive to relaxation and holiday-making. There was a large swimming pool there with Olympic diving towers: 5, 8 and 12 meters high. The lowest was almost double the height of a normal high diving board in a swimming pool. It turned out that I wasn't alone in my fear of heights. There it also appeared that I was not the only one with that kind of acrophobia. And it also seemed that there were more people who sometimes thought it a good idea to jump off the towers.

Surrounding the pool was a deck area with deck chairs, and now and then from here and there were great cheers that could be heard over the whole site, whenever one of our clients or colleagues subdued his or her fear and jumped from one of the towers. I did it too: from the lowest tower, which was enough for me. One must have a certain respect for one's own fear: in the final analysis, it is a warning signal. (One person went beyond his own boundaries, chose a higher tower than he felt good about, and injured himself). For me, it was difficult all over again (it was also higher), and very satisfying, especially with the applause, but it was nothing like the triumph that I experienced as a small boy in Dordrecht. It did teach me that that earlier learning experience would never get lost.

The Message from My Teacher:

I have already mentioned certain important lessons that I learned from this experience. But the most important lesson is this: I learned here to distinguish between my acquired rationality and my "inner source," the deep voice of my conscience, my intuition, and my wisdom (which I called "quiet but nevertheless clear voice inside "). This voice has little to do with what you have learned in this life, but everything to do with the reality beyond the everyday, material world. We have an open connection with this reality, even though for many this connection is blocked or stopped up due to everything that you learned during your upbringing (conditioning). You are, as it were, a channel where the energies of heaven and earth flow, like water through a channel dug in the earth. See the figure below.

The channel

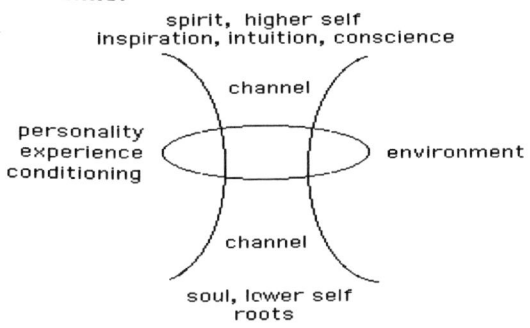

```
                spirit, higher self
           inspiration, intuition, conscience
                      channel

   personality
   experience   (         )    environment
   conditioning

                      channel
                soul, lower self
                     roots
```

The circle in this figure is our conscious self, with which we communicate with the world around us, and where our experience and our conditioning influence our behavior. The channel flows through this circle, and forms on the one hand the connection with our roots which we can learn to be aware of (where we come from, our biological or physical background formed through our evolution; what our connections to the earth and nature are; you could say, our soul), and on the other hand our intuition, our inspiration, and our conscience (to the extent that it isn't conditioned; you could say, our spirit). The analogy with the channel is a bit misleading, because the energy in the psychic canal can travel in both directions. When we open ourselves to this energy, we can grow and break through our conditioning.

We are often so busy thinking and rationalizing that the clutter in our heads prevents us from hearing or experiencing what is passing through the channel. We need to listen a bit more, to become silent. In the beginning we might not hear anything: our inner ears have been trampled on a bit. But if we are patient and attentive, a source of inestimable value will open for us. The form of this source is unpredictable: it comes to one person in words, to another in pictures, intuition, feelings, or a sure and simple knowing. You will certainly recognize this source when it comes: most people already know exactly what I am talking about.

The value of this experience also consists of the fact that once I had heard the source—and even more, had listened to it—it became much easier to get through to it, even though I may not always listen to it. I also recognize more easily the difference between my inner voice and the prejudices of my conditioning and experience.

The Two Generals

Once upon a time there were two generals who—this story took place in an earlier time—stood on a hill looking at an old-fashioned battle. The bullets whistled by their ears, but military protocol demanded that they remain standing there. The first general was fire-eater and stood as calmly as if he was in his garden on Sunday watching the grass grow. But the other was scared to death, and was shaking like a leaf.

The fire-eater said to the other, "Come on, are you a sissy? What kind of general are you? Be a man and take yourself in hand!"

The other said, stuttering, "I-i-i-if y-y-y-you were a-a-a-as afraid as I...I...I am, y-y-you would h-h-h-have been gone a l-l-long t-t-t-time ago."

The Message from My Teacher

This story teaches us something about courage. We can all imagine a situation where courage is required in order to move into it. These are frequently precisely the situations that we must engage in for the sake of our own growth process. Perhaps the iron man in the story would be scared to death to sit down to a dinner. Or to feel his pain, and to share his tears with his wife.

Becoming aware of our own fears—and everyone fears something—makes us gentle in our judgments towards other people. And that makes it further possible to get close to others, to make real contacts, at any time that we wish.

War and Peace

I still remember quite a lot about the war (This of course for me was the second world war). I was born in 1940. My earliest memory dates from when I was two weeks old. But the memory is vague, and I only remembered it in a therapy session, in a state of altered consciousness. I was lying in my cradle and I was cold, because my covers had fallen off. I still see before me the vague contours of the little room I laid in.

But the earliest "ordinary" memory dates from when I was around three and a half. Then I got too near to a litter of puppies, and as a means of warning me, the mother dog bit me in the toe. The dog didn't draw blood, and so there was nothing wrong, but I was greatly shocked, and for a long time—also later—I was scared of dogs. I actually only got over it when I myself came to own and train dogs.

Furthermore, there was still another reason that I so overreacted to the dog. It happened in the house of friends of my parents. My parents had just been, on account of resistance activities and also due to the Jewish origins of my father, arrested. I witnessed that although I myself was not taken away, but instead brought to the neighbors, and that was probably the real threatening experience: so threatening, that I "forgot" it and projected my feelings onto the incident with the dog.

My parents were quickly released, however. My mother was pregnant, and that fact was used by the resistance to secure the release from prison of my mother, and through an administrative "error," also my father. Both went immediately—separately from each other—underground. For my mother, the risk was smaller, and she could live more or less normally, although not at home, but rather by host families.

These were sometimes friends, sometimes strangers. She had me, and later my baby brother, with her, and for a year she changed host families every three months; finally in the fall of 1944 she came home to my grandparents in Amsterdam, and stayed there through the last winter of the war.

I didn't really suffer during the war. The worst was the repeated changing of host families, and the accompanying change of kindergarten and "little friends." It made me feel insecure, and I felt as if I didn't really belong there. I remember only a few incidents from this period, in fact all unpleasant. A ball that rolled under the tram, and that was—at that time—irreplaceable. (I can still see the tram bearing down on me, bells ringing, and me, at the last minute, jumping back—and I can still hear the angry voice of the mother of the host family—at the time you couldn't just go out and buy a new ball). My leg caught between the spokes of the wheel of the bike one time when I was riding behind my mother, that caused me to go around for days with a bandage on my leg and—was that necessary, or simply to comfort me?—with a stick as a sort of crutch. After the first shock, I found this to be terribly important—the children from that host family can still remember it as well. The Philips-bombing, that we lived through under the stairs. Later, in Amsterdam, standing in line in the soup kitchen. The vegetable peel soup and the tulip bulbs that I could hardly force down my throat. (Although it was still always easier than the stringy meat that we got after being liberated. I also remember my mother's anger at the time: at last she could give her child meat, and he didn't want it). An air raid in Amsterdam on the way home from school, when I trustingly and following instructions went and stood in an archway. And one time that I was teased unmercifully by older boys who took my trousers and underpants, and I had to go home with a bare bottom. As small as I was, I experienced this as a great shame.

Room for Happiness

Perhaps I remember all of these incidents because it was in fact not a very pleasant time, and I projected my feelings onto these events.

I also didn't really suffer from hunger during the war. When the food situation got tight, we had extra rations for my brother, who was only one year old, and for my grandfather, who was sick and had a stomach ulcer. Neither wanted the extras, or only a part of them—an egg, a pint of milk, porridge—and then all of that came to me. But I can nevertheless remember how wonderful it was when I got, at half past ten—coffee time—the second bare slice of bread of the day.

The worst was actually the fear. I wasn't directly threatened, and was therefore not actually afraid, but I felt it around me, without my knowing, as a child, precisely what was going on. My mother and my grandparents were truly afraid. Afraid that my father, who was somewhere else underground, should somehow die. After the liberation of Southern Holland, where my father then was, communication was impossible for another six months. He could be in safety, but it was just as likely that he could be dead. Afraid for my grandfather, who became increasingly sick and could die through a lack of good food and medicine (he made it by the skin of his teeth). Afraid for my father's parents and sister, who were underground. Afraid for my mother's brother, who was in prison in Burma. Afraid that the Germans—and the Japanese—would continue to hold out for a long time. It must really have been an enormous disappointment when the Allied attack in South Holland bogged down. There was hunger, and fear of starvation. There was fear of being caught. I remember an identity check in the street. "Come," said my mother. "Let's just go quickly around this other way," as she dragged me towards a back street. Apparently, she was not very secure about her false identity card.

As a child, you don't know really know what hits you. My

mother tried insofar as possible to protect me from misery, and naturally never talked to me about her fears. My grandparents even less. But I felt it all around me. It was a dismal time, and that came out at home as well, since I remember my mother's winged expression: "When the war is over, everything will be good." Then there would be peace, and joy. Papa would come back home. There would be lots of food, and also cakes, and peanut butter, and that kind of thing (I had no idea what that was). We would live in our own house again. When the war is over, then there will be a party, liberation. People will laugh and dance once more. When the war is over...

One day there came a whole lot of airplanes flying low. My brother, was also not insensitive for the fearful atmosphere around him, cried out. But my mother said that these were now friendly planes dropping food packets. It was good to see how happy she was. She obviously knew that it was the beginning of the end. To my brother, then 14 months old, she of course didn't say this. He couldn't be calmed down. He wrecked a moment that should have been great. I hated him. Afterwards, I thought that he came too close to my own unconscious fears. But the food situation quickly improved. I remember the Swedish white bread.

One morning shortly after this I was woken in my small bedroom by my grandparents, and I heard the radio on loud. A voice was speaking loudly and clearly. That was in and of itself unusual, since we listened to the radio in secret and therefore it was usually kept low. My mother came inside. She had tears in her eyes. "It is over," she said. "The war is over." And she hugged me.

And indeed, as my mother had said, everything after the war was just good, or at least much better. There was an atmosphere of relief, and now and then uncontrolled joy. Two weeks later my father stood on the stoop, healthy and well. As a war correspondent for *Het Parool* (*The Word*), he was able to travel quickly. When, shortly thereafter, one of his colleagues teased me, he took me under his protection. I had a *father* again! The food situation rapidly improved even further. My grandfather began to get better and was soon out of danger. My grandparents on my father's side, and my father's sister, appeared to be in safety. We would be able to go back to our own house again. My mother was right: after the war, everything was fine.

Until that certain day—I still know it well—it must have been two or three months after the liberation, that the tragic news arrived. My uncle—whom I had never met—my mother's brother, the beloved son of my grandparents—had died in Burma in captivity. It was terrible for my mother, but worse for my grandparents. They were destroyed. I can still see my grandfather sitting, collapsed, in his chair, a broken man. My grandmother wept silently in front of him, the tears running down her cheeks. She kept saying, "My boy, my boy." No one else said anything.

I had completely forgotten this event, It was only more than 30 years later, in a therapy session, that it came flooding back. With all of the feelings that went with it: the intense sympathy for my grandmother and others, that was more than I could bear at the time. The rage, the childish blaming. But above all, the fact that my mother had lied (that is what it felt like as a child then): after the war, not everything was fine. On a deep, unconscious level, this caused a lack of trust in my mother. I learned then that I could not always take her words literally. (Perhaps it was, therefore, less of a shock for me when I heard that St. Nicholas didn't exist. Somehow, I had already thought something like that). I fear that this also influenced my attitude towards people in general—and a certain distrust is no stranger to me. But the worst was ultimately that this experience undermined my very faith in life: you can't trust life, it is tricky and unfair—that was for a long time my unconscious attitude towards life. In other words, a lack of faith. Now I can tell you, that is not what makes a person happier.

After the war, we had a long period of housing shortage, and an accumulated lack of infrastructure and production factors. That was how we got the reconstruction that actually was completed by about 1953. (I remember then during St. Nicholas time (early December) that I was in a department store, and I saw for the first time the signs of what is now common: people standing in the queue by the cash register for random buying—in 1956 we had our first overspending and had to follow a spending limit).

But the restoration of my faith came about more slowly. As I write this, I am 52 years old, and I am still involved in reconstruction. And I think that I am not the only one. I know for a fact that there are people who have died, and are still dying, for whom this process is far from complete. I think, too, that the disappointments that people experienced after the liberation—it didn't seem, after all, possible to build an ideal society—also has to do with the fact that people tried to leave their earlier disappointment and sadness behind too quickly. In the last analysis, a great many people had terrible war memories: loss of one's beloved, the experience that you can't trust each other; guilty feelings over your own cowardice, fear, and the like. Faith doesn't fall from the sky, and others—or the church—can't give it to us. We can build it up ourselves, but not before we have dealt with our own disappointment and hurt.

This account also holds for people who have other sad or disappointing experiences that have nothing to do with the war. No peace, without working through the war. So we human beings still have a lot to do.

The Message From My Teacher:

No peace, without working through the war. If this is true, it explains many of the dreadful conflicts in the world: in Bosnia; in Palestine; in Ireland; in the former Soviet Union; but also closer by: at work; with your neighbors; with foreigners, and so forth.

Faith can be described as trusting that life will give you what you need. That life will always take care of you. "Do not be anxious about your life, saying, "What shall we eat?" or "What shall we drink?" or "What shall we wear?" For the Gentiles seek all these things; and your heavenly Father knows that you need them all. But seek first his kingdom and his righteousness, and all these things shall be yours as well" (*Matthew 6: 31-33*).

In other words, only concern yourself with the essential values of Life (the Kingdom), then you will be taken care of. A much-read text, especially in the marriage ceremony. But do you believe it? Or have you discarded your trust in Life along with your faith in God?

If you don't have this trust, then it is critical to hold on to what you have: your possessions, your job, your partner, your house, your territory. You are quick to feel threatened. You see the world as a place of scarcity: there is not enough for everyone. There is competition for power, prestige, status, possessions. There is "struggle for life" and "survival of the fittest." There are winners and losers. There is fear of losing what you have. And you tend to rebel against life or circumstances. You make yourself powerless, because you are a victim.

It is in this way that negotiations fail or lead to unsatisfying compromises; that people dig in their heels during conflicts; that peace efforts get sabotaged and wars are fought to their bitter end. That is why it is so important to build up your own faith: the trust that life will give you what you need. That is not easy to believe when your life has brought you pain and disappointments. Life isn't fair, at least not in the way we normally think of fairness. It is clear that there is suffering, undeserved and unwanted, and the sense and the cause of it are frequently perceived only with difficulty. Still there seems to be little relation between the degree of a person's faith and the amount of suffering that has hit him. You might even say that it often is the case that the more faith a person has, the more open he is to the suffering in the world around him, and the less likely he is to close himself off to it. There seems to be a certain relationship between faith and the capacity for compassion and empathy.

In the final analysis, faith is an act and a choice: you choose it or you don't. And if you choose it, it is does not appear immediately, but you can then build it up. You do that not by denying or suppressing your doubts (that only leads to scepticism or self-indoctrination), but simply by not focusing on it. On the contrary, you can focus on the beauty and nobility in yourself or in the world around you (without closing yourself off from the suffering in the world), or you can pay attention to the ugliness in human beings or in yourself. It is a question of choice. The first builds up your faith; the second undermines it.

There is still one more method to increase your faith: be of service. Not because you should, or because you would otherwise feel guilty, or because you would like to get something out of it, but simply for pleasure. Being of service in this way gives so much, the surprising thing is that people don't do it more often: a good feeling about yourself and inside; a great reputation; pleasure; and trust. However, the paradox is that if you do it primarily because of what you can get, it doesn't work so well. Being of service to others is a natural thing to do; it is inherent in your being. It is the lack of faith and trust that has caused you to lose contact with it. On the other hand, being of service is a sovereign remedy to restore

Room for Happiness

debilitated faith. And if you don't sense that, or if you don't believe it, I recommend just simply to begin. The feeling will come later. Encourage someone! Listen really to a friend or a colleague (or your partner!). Give someone a present unexpectedly (for example, this book). Give away something that is dear to you, such as a piece of jewelry or a beautiful necktie. Wash the dishes for the fun of it. Send a blanket to a disaster area. In short: make the world a nicer place.

There is Something About Time

Arriving on time isn't what it used to be. We used to say in school that the bridge was open, or that we had had a flat tire; these days the most common excuse is: "I was in a traffic jam," or, "The train was late." This can in general be taken as disguising the fact that you left home too late.

I am not good at being late. I was as a child. Then I wasn't good at being on time. That is to say good at getting to school on time, but not at getting home. A veiled form of protest, I think. During a certain period I went swimming after school, and I always left the swimming pool too late. Or I stayed hanging around the schoolyard too long—certainly in the marble era, when I still had to make good my losses or consolidate or increase my profits. When I got home I said, even before my mother could open her mouth: "There is something about time..." I didn't have traffic jams available to me then, did I? This became a running gag in the family.

But these days I am not good at being late any more. I don't like it, and so I always leave on time. My girlfriend is just the same. The following story can serve as an illustration.

I had to give a lecture in New York, on a Friday evening at 7:30 p.m. I also had to do a few other things in America, and my girlfriend and I had also decided to add on a few days vacation in New York. However, she couldn't leave any earlier than Friday. I would have preferred to leave on Thursday, to give myself time to acclimatize—no time pressure, and so forth—but Friday was also possible. The plane was scheduled to leave at 10 a.m., and because of the time difference we would be in Kennedy Airport at 12 noon. Even considering that the trip from Kennedy Airport to Manhattan was easily one and a half hours, and that you lose about that much time at the airport—Kennedy Airport is one of the most unpleasant airports in the world, and the passport control there is just about as slow as in the former East Block countries—I could nevertheless be in our apartment by 3:00 p.m. Enough time for a shower and an afternoon nap, so that I would be fresh for the lecture in the evening.

Before leaving, we drew angel-cards. "Love" for my friend—mmm...that was extremely promising—"faith" for me. That triggered in me a vague feeling of anxiety: why should I need to have faith?

We got to Schiphol Airport nice and early, and at 9:30 a.m. we stood by the gate. Alas, as due to a technical problem, the plane would leave later. The expected departure time was now two o'clock, and wouldn't we be interested in coming to pick up a lunch voucher? My friend put her "loving" arm around me, and I did a quick calculation: two o'clock departure, four o'clock arrival—everything could still turn out OK. I opened myself to the Angel of "Faith."

At 1:45 p.m. we were told that the problem was not yet solved, but would we please just wait "standby," since the plane could now depart at any moment. The clock struck two o'clock, two-thirty, three o'clock. I called my secretary and asked her to call the organization in America and to say that I was coming, and to request that they try to hold the attendees for as long as possible. I was supposed to give a workshop the following day, and the registrations were only likely to be dependent on the lecture. Americans like first to see what they are getting, before they are willing to give someone their time, money, and trust. On the subject of trust...I was having the greatest difficulty keeping contact with my angel...

Room for Happiness

Just after 3:30 the boarding began, and at a bit past four we were in the air. It could all still more or less work out. An hour before landing, scheduled for 5:30, I called the organization, and asked them again to hold onto the people. And we were indeed in Kennedy Airport at 5:30, and, wonder of wonders, at 6:30 we walked out the door. The taxi-driver, to whom we explained the situation, was an exceptionally stout American woman who nodded in silence, and thereafter stoically and with true contempt for death hurtled through the traffic, now and then gently displacing another auto, ignoring the shouting match that was created. By improbable routes and back streets she succeeded in bringing us crossways through the New York rush hour, setting us down on Spring Street, in Lower Manhattan, at 7:28 p.m. Whereupon my friend said the memorable words, "I do believe that we are rather poor at being late..." The lecture went exceptionally well, thank you very much, and delivered a good number of participants for the workshop.

What we didn't know at the time was that the airline with which we had flown—TWA—did not have the most wonderful reputation for its service. One week later we had to take the same plane back—scheduled departure at 8:00 p.m. from Kennedy Airport. But "due to a technical problem with the equipment..." (later we learned that the same plane had been flying back and forth between New York and Amsterdam, with delays every day for the same reason, a malfunctioning generator). In short, after many hours of waiting, in the meantime completely emptied airport, where even the drink stands were no longer open, we learned at one in the morning that we wouldn't be able to leave that day, and wouldn't we like to come pick up a hotel voucher? After an hour and a half waiting in the queue—I swear to you, this was America—we landed at 3:15 a.m. in our hotel. While waiting, I had heard that the guarantee that TWA gave that you would be transported the next day was worthless, if you didn't arrange the return flight yourself beforehand. Accordingly, that night I hung on the telephone from 3:15 to 5:00 a.m. to arrange the return. Finally it succeeded, with TWA and Garuda via Paris. Departure: the following day at 3:00 p.m.

Given what we had heard and experienced the night before, I wanted to check in on time; thus, after spending the morning in a desolate Holiday Inn, in an even more desolate neighborhood (there was too little time to go back to New York again) we checked in at 1 p.m., and indeed we departed at 3 p.m. for Paris. Imagine my surprise to find that this plane was half empty, while at least dozens of our fellow passengers from the previous day were still hanging around the airport, because there were no seats to be had on flights to Europe. Among them were teachers who had to start school the next day, and many others who had to be back at work on Monday.

Garuda had a two-hour delay in Paris, so that we finally arrived at Schiphol, with a 27-hour delay, on Monday morning at 11:00 a.m. in place of a Sunday morning at 8:00 a.m. I had had to cancel my Monday morning appointments (but at least I hadn't arrived late). In spite of this, and despite two moderately sleepless nights and jetlag, I felt reasonably fit, and I had a couple of important appointments that afternoon. So I thought: go home for a bit, take a shower, put on clean clothes, and to work. Now, I really shouldn't have done that...

When, at 1:30 p.m., I drove through the Schiphol tunnel for the second time that day, on the way to my appointment in The Hague, I was fast asleep. I have seldom woken up so abruptly. I was woken by a crash, and immediately realized that I had fallen asleep. The car motor wasn't running anymore, but the car was still moving, and with the momentum that I had, I maneuvered it to the shoulder outside of the tunnel. While I was getting out of the car to investigate the damage, an enormous tank-truck stopped behind me. The driver rolled down his window and said, "Mister, what are you *doing*?"

I said, "I was sleeping."

He said, "Should you really be doing that, in the Schiphol tunnel?"

And I again, "Well, now that you mention it, no. I shouldn't have been doing that."

He said, "You scared the hell out of me. I was driving along as if there was nothing the matter, and all of a sudden I heard an enormous crash behind me." He had been driving in the rightmost lane, and I was just passing him and had sailed into his side. Luckily he had a ladder on the side of the truck to be able to climb into the tank. This ladder had prevented me from getting caught under the truck, in which case I would have been history. The silhouette from the support beams in my door was clearly to be seen in the metal of my right front door. I had good luck, you might call it. The man was in fact really nice: he wouldn't take any reimbursement for his damage.

All in all, my car wasn't working anymore. I called the Automobile Association. They came, and within one minute they had the car working again. I did have seven thousand guilders damage, but I nevertheless drove on to my afternoon appointment. Crazy of course. And indeed, I was too late for the first appointment. In contrast, I was precisely on time for the second one. But perhaps that level of rigidity isn't really a virtue in all circumstances...

This suddenly makes me think of a completely different story. Years ago, when I was still a psychotherapist, and also rode horses, I had taken a morning ride through the dunes near Overveen. I came back to the stable and was invited by the stable owner to take a ride on the beach to Noordwijk, to have lunch there, and then to ride back. But I had a therapy group at one o'clock, and so I said that I couldn't go. He said, "What's the point of having your own business, when you're just as stuck as if you had a boss..."

I thought, *I'm even more stuck; if I had a boss, I could have taken a "mental health day."* I loved my work, but I felt it suddenly a duty. Right at that time, I was trying to teach my clients how to learn to follow their hearts. "If your life is ruled by duty," I used to say, "something isn't right. You get too little pleasure, and you end up being full of inner resistance."

And now I, myself, was feeling the conflict between my obligations on the one side and my desires on the other. What must I do now? You can't truly choose for your work and your clients unless the alternative—not choosing them—is also a real alternative. In short, I decided to go with the stable owner. I called the secretary and asked her to say to the group that I wasn't coming, and to recommend that they work without me.

We had a glorious day. It stormed and rained, and we had a wild ride over the beach. At lunch, the brandy flowed, and I succeeded in not having a single guilty moment.

Later, when the group figured out that there hadn't been a single reason for my absence other than my own choice for myself, most of them were initially highly indignant. But in answer to my question if they hadn't done good work, and hadn't gotten a lot out of the group, most could only answer in the affirmative. There were only two group members who kept having difficulty with it. The others had learned, that afternoon, something about independence from me as their therapist and about taking responsibility for their own lives—just as I had taken responsibility for my life—which took them in a single bound significantly further in their therapy. And I had experienced what freedom is in practice; the freedom of the here and now. Experienced in this way, freedom is very close to response–ability, that is, to being ready and able to give a response. I still generally keep my appointments, but I know

now that I do it out of free choice, and not because I say I should, or others say I should, or because it's the right thing to do.

The Message from My Teacher

Both stories are about taking responsibility. Of course circumstances influence our lives. But in the first place: to a great extent we create our own circumstances (through attracting situations, and engaging with them, avoiding them, or getting into or out of them). And in the second place: *we* determine how we deal with the circumstances.

That's why you could say that we are 100% responsible for our own lives. The trick is in fact to take 100% responsibility. The great advantage of doing so is that in any case we can no longer consider ourselves to be victims. We can't blame the circumstances or other people for our misery, not even God or Life. And we can, therefore, if desired, use all our energies to change our own situation.

It is surprising what a beneficial effect 100% responsibility has on communication and cooperation. No excuses, no guilt trips, no need to defend yourself. How efficient! This might just be the most important step towards a world where we treat each other with honesty and respect; a world with peace and love in place of a world of conflict and power struggles.

Having Children

We waited to have children until we were truly ready. We philosophized about what we would rather have first: a boy or a girl. It didn't matter to Maria, but I did have a preference for a girl. That had to do with the fact that my father and I had not had the most intimate contact, and I thought that I would feel somewhat inhibited with a boy and wouldn't find it easy to cuddle him. I also had had, even as a child, little affinity with typical boys games such as soccer and the like. I didn't know if I could be a good father for a boy. So we made love, and Maria got pregnant and it was a girl. A wonder! I will never forget that first night. All of a sudden we were three. Every so often, a soft gurgling sound came from the cradle. Boy were we happy!

About a year later we began to think about a second, and Maria said, ruminating, that it still didn't make much difference, but that she nevertheless now had a clear preference for a boy. And I actually did, too. I was at that time in therapy, and thought that I could overcome my potential inhibitions. And a boy would of course be really very nice considering the composition of the family. So we went to bed and I became impotent. Very humiliating and frustrating. It cost me a half year in therapy and a great deal of shame before I got over it. But then I completely wanted a boy. So we went to bed and it was a boy. I was so glad when he came, and of course I could cuddle him just fine.

About a half year later we thought about a third. I thought, *well yes, I can deal OK with boys, but if it was completely up to me, I would so like to have another girl.* It didn't matter to Maria. So we went to bed—well now, that wasn't the whole story, let's just say that it more or less overcame us one gorgeous day in May—and it was a girl. Which just goes to show that the father determines the gender...

The Message from My Teacher

That is of course a joke. It is certainly the spermatozoa that determine the sex, but the father has no apparent influence on them. It is like throwing a die. If I throw the die, a number comes up, for example a six. You could say that I caused the six to come up, but that I had no influence on it. Or is it different still?

For otherwise, how could you explain that my son won so often at playing the board game "Goose," that the other family members began to lose their pleasure in the game. And how does it come about that some of my friends always win at roulette (I myself can do that pretty well in blackjack). And that without playing any particular system. Is all that just blind fate? Then there must be a certain system in the fate.

When we look back at our lives, there is frequently a certain pattern to be observed. The events have a meaning which we often are unaware of at the time. On account of this, I find that I am not so quick anymore to believe in involuntary fate. I do thoroughly believe that events like those described above and in the next story occur according to an voluntary pattern. Which doesn't automatically mean that you have your life under control, however.

I go into this in greater detail in connection with the upcoming stories in this book (specifically "Wondering," "Charlie," "Cancer," and "Manifestation").

Soccer

Even when he was little—five, six, seven years old—my son always wanted to play soccer with me. I hate soccer. But I had the idea that if he wanted it so much, every so often I still had to do it. But it always ended in drama. He was too quick for me, and I couldn't stand it, and it always ended that I kicked him in the shins. By accident, I swear it...

At that time I attended a summer conference, where I participated in a men's group. And in the men's group we were talking about fathers and sons. This brought me for the first time in contact with what I had missed from my own father, and that was intimacy (later I saw, in photos, that in the beginning of the war, when I was younger than three, that he did still have it then). And with a shock I realized that I was doing the same with Roeland, my son. In spite of the fact that I had worked on this in my therapy around the time of his birth, and thought that I had in fact worked through the issues about the relationship with my father, it appeared to be much deeper, and I appeared to be repeating—in a completely different form—the same pattern. Only through realizing this could the old pain come to the surface, and I wept. It was certainly quite something that I could, since I had earlier learned to control all my feelings, and I hadn't been able to cry between the ages of 13 and 33. In fact, I realized that I was poised to squander the chance to build up an intimate relationship with my son, and thus at a certain level stood to lose him. That moved me deeply. And suddenly I was flooded by the whole soccer drama, and I was able to see that the lack of intimacy between me and my son played a role there, too. But I still didn't like soccer. What to do?

But alas, if you can just release your feelings, you get creative. Suddenly I realized that my son could go to a soccer club. And so we arranged it. And from that day on, every Saturday I stood on the sidelines, and drove my car, full of energetic boys, to the competing soccer team. Sunday evening we found ourselves in front of the tube, and together we gave expert commentary on the contests in the premier league. Later we of course watched the European League, European Championships, and World Championships. We even went to the Olympic Stadium once in a while. That is how I got to like soccer..to *watch* it, I mean.

Our intimacy was of course not only expressed in our joint activities and interest in soccer, but it did prove to be a natural and good start.

The Message from my Teacher:

This story hangs together with the previous one. In that case it becomes less and less likely that the previous story describes purely a chance process. It is perhaps not so that I had the whole process under control, but it in any case makes sense. I create an essential learning experience for myself.

What exactly do I learn? I break through the cycle of the generations (see also the story "In Memoriam Patris" in this book). What you frequently see is that parents—usually unconsciously, and sometimes with the best intentions—damage and hurt their children (as I did in the first part of this story). The children become adults, and sometimes they are aware of what has occurred, and sometimes not. If so, then they want to do better with *their* children. The tragedy, however, is that this seldom works. Conscious or unconscious of what your parents have done to you, you pass the same behavior patterns on to your children anyway. And so a backlog of hurt, pain, sorrow, rage, revenge, and hate builds itself up

Room for Happiness

through the generations, which you are often not conscious of, but which comes out in any number of ways: powerlessness, dissatisfaction, sickness, relationship and communication problems, destruction between you and your children, misunderstanding, fights, and what have you.

The only way to break through this process is to become aware of your own wounds, and to feel and express the pain from them, just as long and as deeply as is necessary. It helps when this occurs in the presence of an understanding listener—as I did in the mens" group—but that is not strictly necessary. However it works, there always comes a moment when you are cried out, and your own self-pity can be transformed to empathy and compassion, both for yourself and for others who have hurt you. Now is the time to forgive yourself, your past, and others: knowing that what is done is done, but you are still alive and can once again grow, bloom, and bear fruit. You are free!!

Breaking through the cycle of the generations is an essential prerequisite for your own inner peace, and also for achieving a world in which understanding and care for each other and for our surroundings play a major part. Because how can you have care and understanding, when you are still so full of (probably unconscious) rage, resentment, and hate?

Skiing

"You've just got to come skiing with me one time," said my friend, Aadt, somewhere around 1980. That seemed like nothing for me. In the first place, I am a zero where sports are concerned. And I thought that downhill skiing would be just the same type of thing as skating. The suffering I endured during skating in my youth swam once again into my consciousness. I was always cold, was always afraid of falling, and furthermore I never made it.

"No," said Aadt, skiing is something completely different. To make a long story short, I let myself be coaxed. Aadt, also not known for being a sportsman, can nevertheless ski quite well, and so went on up the hill. I went with a beginner's class to the practice area. My feet hurt, but I thought it went with the territory, just like in skating.

After the first difficult steps we set out with a side-step to climb up a little ways, and were requested to snowplow down in a curving line. Plow, then turn the downhill ski out; weight on the downhill ski; body towards the down—great, but I couldn't get anywhere near that far. Like a stone I crashed downhill. There was only one way to stop, and that was to fall down.

Actually, on that day I only learned one thing: that falling wasn't as bad as I thought, and that you didn't immediately break your leg. Alas, it didn't lead to my learning to ski the next days. On the morning of the second day the ski instructor considered that the time had come for our class to go up the real slope. I couldn't imagine it, since the hill couldn't be seen from the practice area, and I had watched very little skiing on TV. I had my reservations about it but that wasn't relevant, since after some contact with other ski instructors I was put back a class, and I was once again with the beginners. My old class disappeared over the hill and were lost to sight.

I still couldn't make curves. Only with difficulty could I take the practice lift up without immediately falling out of it (that only happened every so often). Once at the top, I went down or I fell. "Ja, Herr Prag, doch, drehen sie die Ski doch nach die Talseite, ja...also, Schade...versuchen Sie es noch einmal" (please turn your ski downwards, Herr Prag...sorry, a pity...try once more please). I learned in any case that my bindings were well set, since they came open each time I fell badly, and that was approximately once every five minutes. I also learned to put my skis back on again on the hill—later this came in very handy. Hopeless. And the pain that I had in my feet...

I write this down so easily here, but I truly went through hell. Pure helplessness: it appeared that my body—probably out of anxiety—simply didn't do what I wanted. The humiliation in front of my classmates. It seems silly now, but at that moment I thought that learning to ski was the most important thing in the whole world, and if I couldn't learn it, I would carry the feeling of failure around with me throughout my whole life. Of course I considered stopping, but Aadt and my own stubbornness kept me from doing that. He had still managed to learn, why couldn't I, god dammit. Nevertheless, it got difficult when this class too disappeared over the hill in the direction of what was then beginning to seem like the promised land. Moses had at least seen that land. I wondered for myself if I would get even that far. At least I wasn't cold; I had achieved that at least. And the evening meals were also truly delicious.

The third day. And suddenly, by God, I more or less began to get it. It is true that my first turn led to a fall, but it was at least a turn. Thereafter it rapidly got better, and in the afternoon—three cheers—there we went over the hill, towards

what appeared to be a lift upwards. I almost forgot the pain in my feet. We went upwards with a long chairlift. It was glittering weather. But I didn't have many eyes for the beauty of the mountains. I squinted to see what awaited me up above. But up above, it turned out fine. There was a slope, not too different from the practice area; larger yes, but not steeper. We made our perfect curving runs after the ski instructor, and came to stand next to each other on the hill. And then it happened...
Suddenly I was overcome by the beauty of the mountains. For the first time I saw the village that lay below. All around me were fabulous, majestic peaks, gleaming white, with here and the there the dark green of the trees. The incredible blue sky. And a cheer began inside...I had done it, I would learn it! I don't know what moved me most: realizing that the suffering was over, that I had stayed with it, that I would be able to ski and would even find it marvelous, or the overwhelming beauty of the mountains. In any case, I was very happy, and a great feeling of gratitude flowed through me. The tears streamed down my cheeks. My classmates, fortunately, didn't notice this.

And indeed, it was a wonderful vacation. The last day in the week, Aadt and I skied together, and we made a short trip. Many wonderful vacations followed it. During many of these vacations, I was happier than I had ever been. In winter sport vacations I can completely let go of the worries that are always with me. Within one week I am completely refreshed. I have energy again for months. With my vacation partners I am able to relax and have extremely deep contact. I don't know what it is: probably not only the exercise and the beauty of the mountains, but also the purifying effect of the mountain air. Skiing is of course also a unique combination of control and letting go—it does seem that, through skiing, I can also do this better mentally, and that I can in this way free myself from the excessive need to have everything under control. Winter sport vacations have taught me to love the winter, now, remarkably enough, also in my own country, whereas I always used to hate winters like the plague.

Would it have been so rewarding if I had learned more easily, or quicker? Perhaps, but in any case it explains why I intuitively knew that I had to keep going. "You can get it if you really want...but you must try...and you'll succeed at last." So obvious, and yet so extraordinary.

The Message from My Teacher:

You can get it if you really want...that is certainly a major lesson. But you must try...yes, but not all trying is equally effective. You can't make the grass grow faster by pulling on the blades. Effort and surrender in the right doses; being in control and letting go in balance; there is the recipe for a fortunate and creative life. That is perhaps the most important lesson that I have learned from skiing.

In Memoriam Patris

When I was still a psychotherapist, I had a problem. The problem was that I couldn't stand when people—my clients—would willingly and knowingly damage themselves. Willingly and knowingly, "deliberately unconsciously," as my instructor said. The problem was, furthermore, that I couldn't stand it when people didn't *want* to get better, didn't choose for themselves, their lives, their own growth. I have occasionally characterized my attitude as "grow or I'll shoot." I have often put people under pressure, almost forced them to grow (which of course doesn't work in practice). I did surely know that even the grass didn't grow faster through pulling on the blades, but in the case of my clients I still couldn't resist it. And it also helped some of them. Through my pushing and pulling, they got through a stuck point, and are still grateful to me (but I now think that they would have come through in any case). Others tended in the event to be daunted by my behavior. And to this day I still have regrets over this. But why, actually, did I do this? In the end of the seventies, I got an answer to this question.

In January, just after New Year's, Maria and I were scheduled to do a (married) couples marathon. We worked from 10 a.m. until the following day 5 p.m., in one stretch with only a few short meal breaks and a few hours sleep break. We worked with ten couples at the same time: group work, body work, and working on the relationship. This time there was, however, a problem: I got the flu. Postponement was of course possible, but that would last quite a long time due to other commitments. We also knew that some of the couples were really counting on it, and that their relationship was hanging on by a silken thread. Also, we could really use the money. So I asked the doctor for a kill-or-cure remedy. I received it, but expressly "at my own risk."

We did the group, and I believe not badly, but afterwards I was sick as a dog. I was consumed with a sore throat, had a high fever, and I began to stink—I am ashamed to say, but it goes with the story—not only from my mouth but from my very pores.

Apparently I needed to go through a purification process; I had to clean out some old baggage. I lay upstairs, but you could already smell me outside the front door. The doctor came, and, with a grin, said to Maria at the door, "Are you afraid that your husband is rotting away?" Well, it turned out that I had nothing more than a bad quinsy, and antibiotics would take care of it. But I felt miserable, also in spirit. Apparently, the crisis was not for nothing. Maria said, "Why don't you consult a colleague for a change?" And so my English colleague, Ian, who had just come to the Netherlands, came over from Amsterdam, and sat next to my bed. He inspected me for a while and said, "What did you do during Christmas?" And suddenly everything fell into place.

At Christmas, my parents were at our house. That was really nice. Only, with my father you can only have deep conversations about politics, philosophy, or society. It can't get too personal. So I began a conversation about national politics, and expressed my disappointment about a certain action from the socialists (my father was a member of the Labor Party and had been a career politician). Actually, I expressed how dejected I felt about how it was going in the world, and I hoped that he could give me hope and optimism again, as he had always done. And suddenly I noticed that he broke off contact. *My God*, I thought, *he is also disappointed. He is actually just as dejected about politics and how the world is getting on as I am*. And immediately I, too, shut myself off, and began to cover less dangerous territory.

Ian said, "It is high time that you realized that your father can't give you any hope. No other can give you hope; on the contrary, you have truly to develop if for yourself." And when he saw that the deep truth of this had penetrated to me, he said, "Come now, I'll take myself off," and left me as a true friend, in the nick of time, to be by myself.

And suddenly I saw the whole story. How my father, Jewish, on account of his origins and his life experience (the war), was deeply despairing. How his whole life was built up as a struggle against despair. How he laid the foundation, both practical and theoretical, for the Humanist Union, as an antidote against a lack of meaning (which he called nihilism). How he continually convinced his children, his colleagues, and the hundreds who came to him for advice and spiritual support: it is not realistic not to hope. But also: how deep in his being the despair was never dissolved; and how, thus, all his structures were at their base lacking in foundation.

As Paul said, we need hope. Not the false hope of shutting our eyes to reality; not the courage of desperateness; not the hope of rationalization (we can't prove that it is going badly, so maybe it is going well). These kinds of hope give energy to things not going well, and so work against us. No, the hope that we need is anchored in trust: in ourselves, in the people around us and in life itself. No blind trust, no naiveté, but the acceptance, the knowing, that people can live lives of creativity, wisdom, and love. Hope that is an expression of the life force itself. My father lacked this kind of hope, and so did I. And I just kept on trying to get this hope from my father. And from my clients. Grow or I'll shoot! If you don't grow, you are feeding my despair. But you have to feed my hope! You *must* grow, you *must* get happy!

This entire construction collapsed on itself on that late

afternoon in January, when Ian said to me that I must stop longing for hope from my father, and after that walked out again. As a child, you need hopeful parents, and if you have them, you develop your own hope. When you don't have them, you become desperate, like my father, and like me. But I wasn't a child any longer! I could hardly spend the rest of my life going through the world seeking a father or a mother figure who would be able to give me hope. No one could give me hope! And certainly not my clients. I must develop my hope myself! But how? And immediately the answer came: through admitting the despair, expressing it, working through it. Then the little seed of hope that had always lain in the bottom of my soul, could finally sprout and grow. That was just precisely what my father had never done. He had struggled against despair, but in so doing he had given it energy, and the despair had become desperateness.

Many years later I sat by my father's sickbed. He would soon be dead, and lay mumbling in a restless sleep. From the words that I picked up, I could hear that he was making up the score, and setting down what he had done in his life. My mother slept in the next room, exhausted from many sleepless nights. Just before dawn my father woke up, calm, peaceful. The despair was gone: he had apparently worked through it. He was clearly in harmony with himself and with the nature of things. He saw me and put his hand out. At last he no longer needed the barrier: not against himself, not against others. There was nothing to hide, no threatening feelings, nothing. There was no longer any need for a defense structure. All of the blame and resentment that I just about always had towards my father had disappeared, and has never returned. I felt a deep contact, and I am convinced that he felt it, too. I hugged him and said goodbye. It was good.

The Message from My Teacher:

In the story "War and Peace" I talked about faith, and here I talk about hope. What Ian said about hope is also true for faith. No one else can give it to you. You have to develop it yourself; without that, it doesn't work. Like in the expression "Hope moves mountains," and "No life without hope."

If skepticism is a sign of an unassimilated doubt, cynicism is a sign of unassimilated despair. There is a distinction between despair and desperateness. The first is a natural feeling, that is on the way towards hope. The second comes about if you don't see the first. You then become desperate, wildly despairing, until you give up (think here about the connection with the word "desperado"). Cynicism is a petrified and weakened form of this.

Without faith or hope your life, and whatever it is that you create in your life, lacks a firm basis. That is not to say that your life cannot be valuable. But because it is based on a defense against doubt and despair, they cannot be fully seen and assimilated. In so doing you create a precarious balance; a permanent struggle against doubt and despair. This costs a great deal of energy, energy that you need to make your life and the world the way you want them to be.

Therefore, face your doubt and despair; (for example, when you see scenes of misery on television) don't struggle against them; don't give them extra attention, but let them in, so that your faith and your hope can sprout and grow. And as I said before, being of service helps. Not like my father and I did, with the courage of desperation, but simply because it is enjoyable (I certainly *also* found it enjoyable).

Serving begins with yourself. So serve yourself once in a while. *Now*, for example, what could you give yourself in this moment? What do you need?

Crisis

In 1981 Maria had had enough. It was worse than that; she couldn't stand it any more. She was so tender bruised and so disappointed, that she herself couldn't any longer feel if she still loved me.

She said all of this, in tears, in a (married) couples group that we were at that time part of. The group was led by Nadine, a truly gifted therapist. Not taking sides, however, was not one of her virtues. No matter how often she had confronted me with my behavior and the consequences of it, when these were, in her eyes, harmful for me or for my surroundings, in conflicts—also with Maria—she had still always in fact chosen my side. Now she asked Maria what it was that she couldn't stand anymore.

And Maria told. About my perpetually returning gloom, which always lay like a shadow over the family. Not permanent, but nevertheless still continually returning. As soon as you thought that for once you could enjoy something in an untroubled way with each other, my gloom came back like a shadow to ruin it. About my grumbling. My unreasonable aggression that always saw the chance to sour a situation or to blow up small problems to large proportions.

In the past we had talked endlessly about this, and Maria had tried to cheer me up, or to give me back my trust, but that had never helped. For a long time Maria had tried not to pay attention anymore, but now she was at the end of her rope. She could not even feel whether she wanted to continue on with me. Also there had always been a whole lot of good, both between her and me and with the children, but nevertheless she was beginning to feel that the balance was tipping toward the other side. Perhaps the balance had in fact already tipped. She certainly didn't want to continue in *this* way. She came across as extremely convincing, and I knew exactly what she meant. In terms of my way of doing things, she was completely in the right.

Nadine listened, and her eyes, too, filled with tears. "That is terrible," she said to Maria. "I understand you very well. In your place, I would feel and act just the same as you." My world collapsed. The fact that Nadine, who always stood on my side, now suddenly and unconditionally supported Maria; I needed this fact to face the terrible truth. That I was busy destroying everything that was truly important in my life: my relationship with Maria, whom I truly loved; our family; our joy of living. That it was possibly already too late. And in a clear moment of insight I saw that no one else could help me anymore. I must change with my own power. And if I couldn't do this, my life would lie all to pieces. Even if I could do it, it was not certain that it could still come out alright. It wasn't five to 12; it wasn't one to 12; it was precisely 12 o'clock. In chess terms, the timing flag was about to fall.

And in deep despair, I decided there and then to change my behavior. If I felt the gloom and destruction coming up, I wouldn't give in to it. I would focus my attention elsewhere. Irrespective of whether I could do that, and irrespective of whether that could still rescue my marriage, I made the decision that I would in any case do everything that lay in my power to break through this pattern. Because I felt that if I didn't, even if my life lay in rubble, had I not done all that was possible for me, I would also lose my self-respect.

I write this all rather easily, but I can assure you that I was in a situation of complete and utter despair. In all honesty I no longer knew whether everything that I had always wanted and always had stood for was lost, and even less whether I was in fact capable of changing my behavior. All that I knew was that

I would do it if I could.

The six months after that belonged to one of the most difficult periods in my life. Both Maria and I had actually given up all hope; only my decision drove me onwards. And it began to work. Whenever my temper or gloom came up, I gave them no chance. I simply did something else, or directed my attention elsewhere. That sounds simple, but especially in the beginning I had great difficulties with it. But it worked. A half year later it was practically habit, and also less rage and destruction came to the surface, now that I was giving them less energy. They didn't ever entirely disappear, but they played no meaningful role in the ten years following. Then they began to poke up their heads again, but that is another story (see "Dark Night").

After these six months Maria began tentatively to hope again. We began extremely gradually to draw close to each other. Little by little, the old intimacy came back, and it deepened as never before. This period proved to be the beginning of the high point of our marriage. We simply had a fantastic time, full of tenderness, understanding, and passion. We were very happy.

Seven years later we nevertheless decided to end our marriage anyway, but that was for another reason, and although it wasn't easy (it involved giving up the illusion that we would stay together until death did us part, and it was taking leave of a life phase—the phase of the family where we were very happy), it happened in good harmony. By then the children were grown, and were leaving or had already left home. We stopped then, because we felt that that was the best for both of our development. I don't believe that we could have done it so well then had we not earlier taken the risk to completely face the truth and express it.

The Message from My Teacher:

Destruction is a terrible thing (see also "Cindy"). It comes out in one person as ill humor; in another in always wanting to get their way; walking over others; meanness; domination; dictatorial behavior; or playing subtle political games. You sometimes don't know, as "receiver" of this destruction, exactly what hits you, only that it feels really unpleasant.

The destructive person is not happy, even when he (or she) can derive a certain pleasure from his destruction. He actually needs this pleasure, since he is in fact deeply wounded. Only he doesn't know where and how, and also doesn't want to know, since that is too painful. The destructiveness is his defense against the world. It can only be hoped that he ends up in some kind of crisis, like mine, with loving, non-judgmental people around him, so that he has the chance to face his own destructiveness. I am convinced that every destructive person gets (creates) this chance at least once in his life, but many let that chance go by.

Nearly everyone is destructive somehow. It is of great importance to find out what form it takes or has taken in you. That insight can help you refrain from judging a destructive person (you or someone else). In this way you break through the destructive cycle, since judging is in and of itself a destructive process, specifically, a process through which you write others off. You often judge from your own (place of) fear. You don't have to approve of a person's behavior in order to understand and to accept the person behind the behavior. Difficult? Oh, certainly! But who says that life is always easy?

Heidelberg

In 1982 I was offered—via my teacher—the chance to take over a therapy practice in Heidelberg. I had, in fact, my doubts about it. Rationally, I no longer blamed the war on the current generation of Germans, but still I never went to Germany on vacation, avoided traveling through it whenever possible, and, when I absolutely had to, I felt extremely uneasy. I was oh so tolerant, but summers in a Dutch seaside resort Zandvoort I still heard the words "damn Boches" repeating in my head. I am half Jewish, and during the war I had my share. I delayed the decision as long as possible, until my teacher said, "*Now* I have to know," at which point I said yes. Adventure beckoned, and I did feel that there was a chance that I could learn something.

So I traveled once per month to Heidelberg. At that time I had a long, large weekend group (more than 30 people) and before the group I did a number of individual sessions. Everything went fine. Germans turned out to be ordinary people with ordinary problems and ordinary feelings. But my crucial experience was still to come.

One day a woman stood up in the group (that was the custom there whenever you wanted to put something on the agenda). She was a gorgeous, slim, tall, blond woman—a "noble Teutonic" flashed through my head—and she said, "I want to work with the following. My parents were convinced Nazis. So I have to judge them as bad. But I loved and still love them. They were the ideal parents to me. How, then, can I believe that they were bad? And still another thing. Their opinions are also inside of me. I drank them in with my mother's milk. I can hear these opinions in my head. There is also a Nazi inside of me. I have been taught that that is bad. I have to believe myself bad. That has worked pretty well. But there is still a protest inside of me. How can I believe myself to be bad on account of opinions that I got from my beloved parents? No matter how it is, I have always kept these feelings hidden. I have never spoken with anyone about them, not even with my friends or with my boyfriend. That is impossible in today's Germany (this was 1982, later it became better - EvP). We have no past. It is taboo to talk about it. For sure when it has to do with something as personal as this. But I can't stand it any longer. I *must* talk about it." A deep silence fell.

Oh my God, there you go, I thought, and I noticed how I pushed away my personal feelings, but at the same time how I opened myself up to my inner source. I very seldom pray, but in that moment I made a quick prayer for spiritual guidance. It was immediately heard.

"I have a proposal," came out of my mouth. "I propose that you now give a speech, as a real Nazi. Tell us what value there is in the Nazi heritage, what a shame it is that that time has so little influence on the present, how tragic it is that Hitler died—but perhaps he is still alive, and that is what you base your hopes on."

Well, she looked at me oddly, and had difficulties to begin. I gave some sample sentences, like, "God, I look back with such longing towards the blooming of Nazism. That was a time when there was still hope for the greatness of Germany. There was attention for the purity of our people, and we didn't shrink from taking powerful measures to conserve and advance that purity." And so forth. She got going.

"Wait a second," I said. "Will everyone in the group who, in their heart of hearts, agrees with her, please go and sit behind her, and the others, who don't agree with her, or for whom this calls up resistance or even disgust, please sit across from her." To my surprise, the group split itself precisely in two.

She gave her speech. Fantastic. There is no other word for

it. My feelings were not yet so closed that I didn't feel the shivers running up and down my spine. Proud, fiery, and absolutely phenomenal, she gave flaming witness to the benefits of national socialism. We listened to her breathless, and under her influence we became, like the audience of the late Herr Hitler. At the close, she received a spontaneous round of applause from the people behind her. An uneasy silence fell. My inner guide took over once more.

"I would like everyone to stand facing each other, the group that is behind her on one side, the group facing her on the other side. And then: let out the stops. Say everything that you have to say to the people across from you. From your feelings. Do what you have to do. There is only one restriction: don't touch each other. No bodily contact. For the rest, you may do anything: scream, nag, ridicule, but whatever you do, get it out."

The room erupted in absolute pandemonium. I have never seen anything like it. Years of frustration, suppressed pain and rage, grief, hate, broken love, despair, doubt, impotence, disappointment—it all came out. (Later it turned out that relatively many of the group members had had parents in the German resistance, or had lost their parents or their house in the war). It was an unbearable racket. I sat numb, but alert, in my chair. Across from me I vaguely saw my assistant, shocked, but still present. Twice we had to hold people apart when they threatened to hit each other. All this went on for perhaps twenty minutes. Can you imagine that? That is incredibly long for that level of intensity. Nevertheless, it drew to a close, and the noise diminished. It became quiet; the quiet only disturbed by a single sob. I took the floor again.

"Now, look at each other, and let yourself be guided by what your heart tells you. If you want to make contact, good. If not, also good. Stay with yourself. Do what feels good."

And very timidly, very hesitantly, contact was made. Here

and there, people began very softly to weep. From relief, but also from grief for all those wasted years. The pain could now come out, but in a soft, melting form. Love and tenderness took over. Friends who had stood on opposite sides—yes, even partners in a permanent relationship—restored contact and bridged the gap of years. People stroked each other, or simply sat quietly next to each other, deep in thought. Hear and there a laugh could be heard. A deep calm settled over the group. I opened my heart and cried, and told the group some of my war experiences, told them about my hatred of Germans. They listened, and a single group member put an arm around me.

We talked about it for a long time; setting down experiences, sharing life histories. And so we healed, in the fall of 1982, our war wounds, and the wounds from those who had not even experienced the war. And you know what, since then I am glad to go to Germany. There are still some remnants of the old thoughts and feelings, but that is no longer important. Some Germans irritate me; sometimes I find them ridiculous. They are a lot like Dutch people. They are like me. I like them.

The Message From My Teacher:

What this story shows is how important it is to forgive, but also what is necessary to be able to do that. You cannot forgive the other until you have felt and accepted your own pain and rage. And make no mistake: the pain and rage are *also* present in us when we—objectively seen—have a less dramatic past than these Germans. I don't know a single person that has nothing or no one to forgive. In the words of the "Transformation Game," "I forgive myself, I forgive my past, I forgive everyone, I am free."

Forgiving sets you free, free from the constricting bounds of the past. The energy that is tied up in rage and resentment becomes available for creativity and love. A burden falls from our shoulders. We can create the future, not as an extrapolation of the past, but as truly new.

Cancer

There is a theory that says that we, ourselves, create our own reality. Completely. That there is nothing in our present situation that we, ourselves, *consciously or unconsciously*, have not co-created or attracted. Not that we always understand *how* we do it; and certainly not that we understand *why* we create things which we would ostensibly never choose. Moreover, this theory is frequently abused as a new kind of guilt-and-punishment ideology, or as a mistakenly understood theory of karma. For example, when someone is very ill, to say, "Yes, you actually did that to yourself. It is your own fault." Or, "That is the negative karma that you have accumulated in past lives, and now you have to pay for it." Complete nonsense. What do we know about it?

This doesn't detract from the fact that I find the theory itself, freed of its Calvinistic trappings, extremely attractive. I had made this theory rather uncritically my own. It is also so tempting to believe that we create life itself, and that the universe is more than a chance, chaotic thing without much meaning. I therefore believed that I made my own reality...until I got cancer.

For years I had had a lump in my groin, and I had had my doctor look at it several times. He didn't see it as serious, and so the lump sat there for years. Until suddenly, in 1985, it began to grow. Without worrying too much, I nevertheless still felt uneasy about it, and so I went back to the doctor—in the meantime a different one. This one also thought that it was no problem, but said, "Let's just remove it and test it. We can better be sure." So I went to the hospital, where they cut out the lump under local anaesthetic in the polyclinic. I could go home immediately. One week later, on Friday, I had to phone for the result.

But on that Friday, they asked me to come in Monday for an appointment. Amazing how a person can suppress their negative expectations. Then of course I knew how late it was. And my wife Maria knew, too. Nevertheless, I said to Maria that Monday morning, "Probably nothing is the matter. If there is something, I will call. If you hear nothing, there is nothing to hear." But there was in fact something. It was cancer.

"How great is the danger, Doctor, what is my prognosis?" Well, he couldn't say exactly, it wasn't his specialty; it could end up alright, but he couldn't be sure of it. He was very friendly but also very serious. He extracted a promise from me to call the Antoni van Leeuwenhoek hospital (a cancer specialized clinic) in Amsterdam for an appointment immediately. He would write a referral; I could pick it up at the hospital on the way to Amsterdam. Clever man; in this way he could check that I would in fact go soon.

I still remember well how I drove home from the hospital. Shocked, but still more or less numb. *Now I have also joined the club*, I thought. *Cancer, now I have it too*. I felt no fear. Under stress, our neuroses come out. My neurosis is arranging, working, controlling. That is just what I began to do once I got home. First I called Maria at her work. "I was not supposed to call if nothing was the matter. But I am calling." Silence on the other end. "So it is cancer, but it can still come out OK." Tears. "Should I come and have lunch with you?" So we agreed on it.

I began arranging. Call the Antoni van Leeuwenhoek hospital and make an appointment. Cancel my appointments for that morning. Call the other hospital to say when I would pick up the referral. Made some telephone calls that I had to do anyway. By 10:30 I had really nothing more to do. Everything was under control. Well, OK, everything except my disease of course...disease? But I didn't feel at all sick! Suddenly the truth began to penetrate: I wasn't sick, but I was in mortal danger! I still remember that lunch with Maria and her friend and colleague quite well. There were yummy sandwiches, many tears, and, remarkably, laughter. The way I came in became later a running gag in the family: "So, how about lunch for my cancer." Yup, your neuroses come out under stress: cynicism.

The reception in the Antoni van Leeuwenhoek hospital was thoroughly fabulous. I had associated hospitals with waiting, endless waiting. In that place, I learned that it can be otherwise. I came into the waiting room for new patients. A volunteer offered coffee, but I could scarcely drink it up before I was called for some administrative procedures. And directly after that to the doctor. He read the referral clearly out loud—great, nothing behind your back!—and made no attempt to cushion it. "This is a form of cancer that doesn't metastasize very quickly, but when it does, it is fatal. We don't yet know what is the matter with you. We will be able to say more only when the operation is done." And be began to describe in detail exactly what they would do: cut away the surrounding tissue; and irradiate in order to kill any of the malignant cells that might be left behind. And now first tests, ending up with an appointment with Harry, the person who scheduled the operating room. It must be done at the end of next week. "But next week I am supposed to go on a winter sport vacation. Could it wait until the beginning of the following week?" That was possible. Was he thinking: perhaps it is his last winter sport? When all was said and done, possibly.

And then the tests. "You will now go through the first circuit, as we call it here." He laid it all out in minute detail. Businesslike, but nevertheless, solicitous. Lung x-ray and lung function test. Laboratory. ECG. Operation appointment. Nowhere any waiting. Everywhere friendly people. An hour later I walked out the door. So it *is* possible to do it like that. For the first time, I felt a feeling rise in me that would never leave me in the coming months: gratitude. Because this is all there. For insurance that pays for everything for you; that it is all arranged like that in this country. That people are loving. That a hospital can be loving. That life is dear and that in any case there were yet months given to me.

Four days later, I stood on the ski slope in Italy and wept. Not from grief, but because I was moved. That life could be so wonderful, skiing so thrilling, the landscape so beautiful. I felt myself to be privileged, because my disease had helped me to experience everything so intensely. Seldom have I enjoyed anything as much as that winter sport vacation. And that in spite of the fact that enjoyment had never exactly been my strong point.

About a week later, I was received in the ward. Again no waiting, but reception by the nurse in charge. "Sir," she said, and looked penetratingly at me. "We have two rules here. Rule one: we always tell the truth here. So if you don't want to know something, you had better not ask it. Rule two: we always tell everything to the patient himself, not to the family. So if *you* want to know something"—and she looked at my wife—"you have to ask the mister here." So, nowhere pity. Nowhere patronizing. Responsibility lies with the patient. Businesslike and careful and attentive. Love. There is where I learned what love is. She said further that there was a general practitioner on the ward, who could always make the time free and who was completely informed as to all the medical aspects. "Direct your questions to her if you want to know more, in place of to the specialist," she said. "He has so little time." There was also a social worker. And there was clergy. "What a country, what a country, where everything is just possible," as one of our national songwriters sang.

I was shown the linen closet and the cold drink chest. "Be sure to put what you want by your bed; tomorrow you won't be so mobile anymore." Where to find the telephone, and how I could call my office when I was ambulatory, and how to ask for it when I lay in bed. Nowhere patronizing. Nothing of being just the patient. I was simply seen as a whole person. That day, I could go wherever I wanted to, as long as I let someone know where I was, so that the doctors could find me. And they came during the rest of the day. The surgeon, who wanted to take one more good look. The radiologist, who wanted to see "before my colleague cuts, because those surgeons, they so often make such a mess of it, that I no longer know where it was." The GP, who did some speedy research and came to make my acquaintance. And another surgeon, "I'm dreadfully sorry, but the program has been altered. My colleague must do an urgent operation tomorrow, in an area where he is a specialist, and so I will operate on you. I hope that you won't take it amiss, but now you have to take off your clothes again—I want a quick look." Nice guy, to apologize like that. And late in the afternoon the anaesthesiologist came. How did I want it? Did I want a sleeping pill? Did I want to be alert or sleepy when I went into the operating room. I began to feel myself an extremely important person, a king for whom everyone made themselves available. Nowhere patronizing. Now I also understood why I had needed to arrive the day before the operation.

I enjoyed those few days in the hospital. A half hour after the operation I was completely awake. I felt fit. Just wanted to eat lunch. My hospital room, which I shared with two others, was a sea of flowers. I believe that there were at least 20 bouquets. I hadn't realized how many people truly loved me, but from the cards it was very apparent that the flowers were no formality. I enjoyed the reggae music on my walkman, music that my son had taped for me. It went through my heart and soul. I had time to think. A client of mine, also a cancer patient, gave me a book: *Getting Well Again* by Simonton and Simonton. I talked to the other patients. With most of them I had immediate contact, much deeper than you normally have with strangers. A heart to heart connection—there in the hospital I learned what that means. The disease had made us all open, especially towards each other. The masks fell away. I saw there how the world can be, and I believe that it *can* in practice be like that.

And I discovered something else remarkable. I could see and feel which of us would get well, and which were likely to die. You could feel it in their energy: it seemed that some had decided to live, and others to die. Simonton and Simonton also write about this in their book.

Getting Well Again was an enthralling book. He was a radiologist, she an organizational psychologist, just like me. He came home one day from the clinic, tired and despairing. "I don't understand it at all," he said to his wife. "We have two patients there; same disease, at the same stage. For one, our treatments are working fantastically. Her tumor is disappearing, healthy cells are hardly ever harmed, and the patient is healing and we will never need to see her again. For the other, everything goes wrong. The tumor doesn't disappear; healthy cells are harmed by the radiation; the cancer metastasizes, and the patient will die. Just how is that possible?"

"Oh," said his wife, "that is easy. I wish you had come to me earlier about this, since that happens to be my specialty: motivation. The one is motivated to live, the other not."

It turned out to be a bit more complicated than that, but that was nevertheless an extremely fruitful point of departure. Building on that idea, the Simontons had done wonderful work. Their help for people with cancer came around to the idea that these people must become aware of the feelings behind the cancer, including the struggle between the zest for life and the longing for death. These two are, according to what I believe, in all of us, and cancer patients, generally gravely ill, have a special way of dealing with them. What is the first thing that cancers patient often say when they first hear that they have cancer? "I don't want to die." In place of "I want to live." But whatever you do, whether you "choose" death, or you "choose" life, that is OK, as long as you make your peace with it.

I had lots of time to think in and after the hospital. I did the exercises from Simonton and Simonton to support my own healing process. After four days I was out of the hospital (it was predicted for eight days—my wife was speechless with surprise). "Can I work during the radiation treatment?" I asked the doctor. "Physically, probably you can," he said, "but don't underestimate the stress. For some people the radiation in itself is a threatening experience, and you will be seeing gravely sick and deformed people." But I continued fully working—in the last analysis I had no permanent job, and the money had to be earned—in spite of the fact that for six weeks I needed daily radiation treatments and that I had appointments and conferences throughout the whole country. (This was in part thanks to the extreme flexibility of the workers in the radiation division, who tied themselves in knots to adapt to my schedule—the darlings!). I was irradiated in the groin, and they expected severe skin damage. Not my skin—up until the last the radiological therapists were still placing their bets. My disease made me choose: I wanted to live.

Do you *really* create your own reality? My first reaction when I got cancer was, "Yeah, but I didn't do *this* myself. Why would I?" But my next reaction was, "Wait a minute: why don't I take this statement simply as a working hypothesis? Let me now for once assume that I *do* create my own reality—how and why have I (unconsciously) done this now in this way?"

This way of thinking appeared to be very fruitful: the answers came to me as a revelation. It taught me how painful I had found a previous experience in my life, and how this experience had deprived me of nearly all my lust for life. It taught me how I didn't yet, after 25 years, love myself enough to take my own desires seriously. For example, I had been walking around for 20 years with the idea that I wanted to go on vacation in the spring, to the south in general, and specifically to Tuscany. But I never did it. There was always something. *This* year I had to take exam; *that* time the children had to be in school; *that* time my clients needed me again; *then* I had to meet my income goals precisely in that time; etc. Did I ever truly listen to myself? That spring, even though my budget was slimmed down through the disease, and in spite of the fact that I once again needed to make my income and I got a terrific work offer that I had to turn down, I went to Tuscany and Umbria. In a church in Assisi I got a deep spiritual experience, that laid a further basis for faith and gratitude for what life had to offer me. Maybe that was why I had to go to this place in the world. In the meantime my prognosis had become much more favorable—no cancer cells were found in the surrounding tissue.

My disease taught me things that I already knew intellectually, but that I had not let get through to me. I wonder if we humans are in fact able to learn without crisis. Theoretically that must be possible, but I see it seldom happening in practice. For that matter, my learning process is still continuing, now as I write this, five and a half years later, just after my last check-up, where I was declared to be cured. I don't have to return anymore. I said goodbye to the Antoni van Leeuwenhoek House where I had encountered so much warmth, and that became for me a spiritual home. Perhaps I needed my disease to be able to learn and to know at a deeper level, and that is why I created it. It was a rich time. I wouldn't have missed a second of it.

After a few months, when the danger was mostly past, my

19-year-old daughter said to me, "Pop, I understand that it was a very critical experience for you, and that you have learned a lot from it. But could you please choose a less spectacular route in the future." That came as a shock to me. Of course they were worried to death. And I had paid hardly any attention to it—in the beginning a bit in relation to my wife, but that too was quickly over. How limited my love for my nearest was and is. I also learned *that* from my illness.

The Message from My Teacher:

Nowadays it is the fashion—particularly in New Age circles—to know precisely where cancer comes from. So as: it is caused by resentment, or according to someone else, by despair, or by whatever; and you do it to yourself. Thus you can also heal yourself, thank you very much. If you don't get better, then you apparently don't want to, or in any case you are not aware enough of what is going on in you. I barely manage to avoid this type of reasoning. What are the facts?

One: Scientific research has determined that cancer breaks out relatively frequently after a serious, shocking experience or after a very difficult period. Apparently the immune system, which in healthy people can destroy and expel deviant cells, has been harmed. This can also result in getting ulcers, shingles, or even the plain old flu.

Two: Scientific research has also determined that miraculous cures can take place. So-called incurable cancers in a terminal state can disappear in an "inexplicable" manner. In any case, what you can see is that people in whom this occurs also go through a major spiritual transformation. (You can't reverse the logic: some people go through a major spiritual transformation and still don't get well. For example, Treya Wilber in the book by Ken Wilber, *Grace and Grit*, see references at the end of this book). That is to say: they come to a different perception of themselves and of life. You see something similar in the case of people who have gone through near-death experiences or other kinds of existential crises.

Three: There are a number of factors which are known to increase the chances of a miraculous cure, or generally, the chances for healing. One of these is the presence of loving support. It is clear how important support is. The position of the supporters is very difficult (see Wilber again): usually all of the attention goes to the patient while the supporter naturally also experiences a great deal of grief and tension.

This allows us to conclude that the psychic and spiritual component of the disease is definitely present, and that it is also very good to direct the attention towards it. Even if these components comprise only 20% of the process, becoming aware of them might just make the difference between living and dying, or, even more importantly, between inner peace and (unbearable) suffering (in the case of either living or dying).

A book that—apart form Simonton's—also presents a balanced and very helpful view on living with cancer is the book from Bernie Siegel—see references again. Suggested reading not just for patients, but for their family and friends as well.

The next story shows where it can lead if we are too rigid in our thinking about this and imagine ourselves to be all-knowing and all-powerful.

Charlie

*"Where were you when I laid the foundation
of the earth?"*
— Job 38:4

Nadine, the therapist with whom I was in therapy at that time, an American, had also had cancer. In New York, she had been in a cancer workshop: people who were working through their disease and trying to get better. Charlie was also a member of this group.

When Charlie got cancer, he was not a nice person. He was hard and merciless. By this I mean that he walked over everyone and everything, just to be able to defeat others. He didn't want to be a loser, and at that time he sure wasn't one. He was successful in business and he couldn't be bothered with these he had beaten. He said that he did all this to provide for his wife and children, but his wife was there to satisfy him and he didn't actually see his children.

His cancer was a dangerous kind. I have by now forgotten what it was, but he was very sick from it, and had to suffer radiation and chemotherapy, and there was only a small chance that he would survive.

His sickness brought his life to an abrupt halt. He made the acquaintance of the cancer workshop, and began to realize what was going on in his life. All the things that he had given up to achieve what he wanted to achieve, and what had now nearly slipped through his fingers. How he had been driven forward by a need to escape a deep feeling of being lost and afraid, and neither loved nor respected by his parents, because he didn't want to feel anymore. How he—unconsciously—thought that if he could only gather enough power and riches, he could no longer be hurt and no one could harm him. How he had transformed his fear and despair into rage and combativeness. And how this energy was now affecting his body. His "spiritual cancer" had become a bodily cancer. And no matter how much he said and thought that he was doing all of this for his wife and children, the awful truth penetrated; he was involved in doing exactly the same thing to his wife and children that his parents had done to him.

Not that Charlie saw all of this at once. He spent a long time defending himself against the feedback that he received from others, and against the insights that the illness thrust upon him. Without the disease, it would have taken ages before the truth got through to him—perhaps never. But he finally broke, and cried deeply and long from pain and regret for all the lost years. In despair he wondered if there was still time for him to give his life a radical new direction. But along the way he became convinced that that could in fact be possible, if only he truly wanted to change. Charlie didn't realize this himself, but wrestled with the same problem as the friends in the Bible story of Job: It can't happen that I continue to be punished if I thoroughly improve my life?

Life seemed to prove him right. Whether through his deep remorse or through chemotherapy, Charlie got better. His rage disappeared, and he used his combativeness for restoring his body. He took up his work again, but in a totally new way: with care for people and with time for his family. His wife and children renewed their contact with him, and Charlie's warmth and tenderness came out. After the heavy storm and rain the sun broke through. Charlie and his family began to be happy, and Charlie thought, *just look, if I am caring, not aggressive and not negative, the destructive energy will not destroy my body either*. And he began to see fellow patients as people who were acting destructive with themselves and their surroundings,

Room for Happiness

and who had it in their power to "see the light" and to get well. No matter how gentle he had become through this process, he nevertheless began to judge his fellow humans again. However the categories were no longer "winners-losers," (winners are good, losers are bad), but instead "positive-negative." People who used there energy positively were good, those who used their energy negatively were bad.

Poor Charlie! This thinking turned against him in a dreadful way, when his cancer came back. Guilt and penance. "I have failed, Nadine," said he to my therapist, then a friend of his, "I have failed terribly. I didn't go deep enough in my self-examination, and my destructiveness came back. And now I am harming my wife and children even more." And he cried with great remorse.

But Nadine said, "Listen here, this is absolute nonsense. You have done what you could and more. That had its effect, also on your disease. It gave you time to do what you still needed to do in this world, and to give what you still had to give. You will leave that behind for your wife, your children, your friends. However, it is arrogant to think that you have your own life *completely* under control. Responsibility, yes, but control? Rather be gentle and loving towards yourself and leave this horrible self-blame behind." Charlie nodded, and later he died peacefully. He had forgiven himself and reconciled himself with life and death.

Several years later, Nadine faced a difficult decision. She couldn't accept the situation in the organization where she was then working, and actually felt that she needed to quit. However, she had three children to support, and shrank from for the social consequences. Then in trance she received a letter, signed, Charlie. In the letter, Charlie asked her to guard her integrity, and to act from it, even when it appeared to be the most difficult path. That led her at that time to quit and to come to Europe. Had she not done that, I would never have met her, and would not been able to learn from her what I needed to learn (specifically, to guard *my* integrity). Could I still have learned that from someone else? I don't know—intuitively I believe not, or only much later. In that case my path would have gone in a different direction. Amazing, the roads we take, and how our paths meaningfully cross each other. They are not by chance, or at least I don't see it that way.

The Message from My Teacher:

It is open to speculation whether the above-mentioned letter truly originated with Charlie, or if it is a product of Nadine's own unconscious mind. But that is not important. In both cases it appears how valuable Charlie was for Nadine, and thus actually gave back to her what Nadine had given him: loving feedback.

If someone gets cancer—or some other disaster occurs—you often see three possible reactions (which also can interact with or follow each other):

-acquiescence, resignation, giving up
-fight
-surrender

In the first instance you are a victim. Something terrible has happened to you, and you can't do anything about it. You are at the mercy of the fates. You can complain "Why me?" or you can just passively resign, but that doesn't make much difference. Obviously this is a poor precondition for healing, and also a poor point of departure for dying peacefully (a feeling of dissatisfaction and resentment remains).

In the second case, you take on the fight. That can be very heroic, and very beautiful, and sometimes also rather effective.

But the battle is coupled to great pain and suffering, and also the effectiveness is not as great as it could be, since fighting someone or something gives energy to that someone or something. In the case of cancer: you win or you lose (and the chance of losing is great), but even if you win, you lose a part of yourself, not only the cancer, but also the part of your personality that is connected to the cancer. Some part of your power also lies in that part of your personality. In this case, it is as if you have been amputated.

The third case—that of surrender—is different. You know that you are yourself the co-creator of your cancer. You don't judge yourself for that, but you face the fact, and finally accept it (first level of surrender). At the same time you realize that you are only a co-creator. Something is going on that is larger than you (comparable to the first step of the 12-step program in Alcoholics Anonymous: it is stronger than I am). You face the problem in its entirety and know that the outcome is uncertain. You attempt not only to accept this, but also to appreciate it. You attempt to say, from your heart: this is good, this gives me what I need, I am grateful for this (trusting in life, which I earlier called faith). This is the second level of surrender. It's called embracement. That doesn't have to exclude you from desiring to live further, but also it doesn't automatically include it. It is in and of itself a separate thing (see also Simonton, Siegel and Wilber).

But whatever reaction you or someone around you chooses, try not to judge yourself or others for it. That is the last thing that we need in that type of situation. What we *do* need is unconditional love. This love means that we accept our own choice and that of others, even though we have our own feelings about them and also express them. If it has to do with someone else, it is good to realize that *we* have *our* feelings, and *he* or *she* has *his* or *her* life, and they also have the freedom to do what they want with it.

Miracles

In the spring of 1987 I didn't feel so great: tired, somewhat listless, less energetic than I was used to, and with less pleasure in my work. I took myself to Marion, a woman who had earlier helped me with healing of my cancer. She "saw" me, and said that I had too much junk piled up in my organism, bodily and spiritually, and that I needed to let myself be purified through the sun and the wind. I had to get outside more, in nature, and to let the sun and the wind play through me. "But I already go outside regularly," I said.

"Yes, but then you go around thinking about everything," she said. "That is not opening yourself to the sun and the wind." That was true.

A couple of days later I played tennis with my good friend who lives in Portugal, and actually lacks a good sparring partner there. And not here in the Netherlands either, with the exception of me. We both play with moderation, but both of us are the same degree of good—or bad—so that our games are always exciting and pleasant. Unfortunately, after half an hour of play, I got a tennis arm, but I thought that it would be such a disappointment for my friend to stop at that moment, that I played on for another half hour, for better or worse. I shouldn't have done that (or perhaps in fact it was better that I did, given what followed, but that depends on how you look at it); since after that I nearly passed out from the pain. That is, if I moved my arm at all. I couldn't even lift up a coffee cup anymore.

I had no time left to go to the doctor, because the next day I had to leave for a conference in Findhorn. Findhorn is a world-famous spiritual community in Scotland; not dogmatic, but affiliated with the tradition of Christian mysticism. Not a sect, but an open community, whose activities included organizing workgroups and conferences. This conference was called "From organization to organism," and had to do with the kind of organizations that are needed in this time.

I enjoyed Findhorn a lot, and the conference was very inspiring. At the opening, we were each requested to take an "angel-card," to symbolize the energy that you could get and radiate outwards during the conference. I drew the angel-card "purification," which at the very least was a remarkable coincidence.

Later that week I was in the bookshop, because I thought it would be nice to take something with me as a memento of Findhorn. But *what* should I take? At that moment I was a little tired of reading, so I remember saying, "I will take a little book." And as if of its own accord, my gaze fell on a little pamphlet that was so thin that there was no title on its spine. "*That* must be it," I thought. I opened it and my eyes fell on a passage: "Purify yourself through the angels of the water, the sun, and the wind." It appeared to be the Essene Gospel of Peace. The same message again, and from a completely different direction! I had just better listen, I thought to myself.

In the conference, there was a "chiropractitioner," a sort of bone cracker, who gave a workshop about spiritual healing. That's were I went. He showed how he used to treat people. He let someone lie on the treatment table, and demonstrated how everyone actually has a crooked spine, which can be perceived when you are lying down from the fact that your legs are not exactly the same length. A crooked spine can lead to back problems and fatigue, and therefore needs to be corrected. He did that first in the traditional manner—with his hands.

After that he showed us how it could be done differently,

with spiritual energy (his name for it was "Christ Energy"). When he did this, you could see the back suddenly straighten (the legs became the same length) without his so much as touching the client. "Much more efficient," he said, "and also much more sustainable. It stays in the right place for a much longer time than if I do it by hand. But you of course also have to change your bad movement habits, otherwise it will go back to being crooked later." Amazing!

At the close of the workshop I went to him and brought up the topic of my tennis arm: I still couldn't do anything with it. "Is it sprained, or is it only out of alignment?" I asked. He looked at it, from some distance, without touching it, and said, "It is only crooked." He made a motion. "But not any longer," he added. And indeed, the tennis arm was cured. No pain any more, and I could fully use it again. "Be a bit careful with it at first, you know," he continued. "It will remain vulnerable for a few weeks more. You also need to discover what you did wrong in playing tennis, otherwise it will come back when you play again." That indeed became clear to me later, but in the moment I was overcome with wonder.

This conference gave me back my belief in miracles. Not only the miracles of nature (the birth of my children, the unfolding of a flower, the development of an embryo, the infinity of the universe), but also those miracles where the laws of nature as we know them apparently do not hold. But even more than that, this experience gave me back my hope and trust. For me, miracles show us something of the reality beyond this world (the world of time, matter and form). These experiences brought me a step closer to the perception that there is a life greater than my own finite life, and that my awareness will not be lost when I die.

At the end of the conference we were invited to make a commitment to a next step of action, in order to build on what we had learned in the conference. Nothing came to me, and I also didn't want to force it. On the way back, however, on the boat, in the cabin that I shared with my friend Wilbert, my next step was revealed to me. Wilbert told me that he had bought the book *A Course in Miracles*, and that he wanted to do the "course." Suddenly I knew with great certainty what there was for me to do: to buy the book and do the course together with him.

And that is how it happened, to the benefit and joy of us both. Two years later I had read the book and had more or less done the course. This deepened my learning process enormously, and has had a great influence on my life and work. But I am far from finished with the course: the learning process continues to the present day.

Manifestation
I

"You definitely must attend the workshop, 'The Art of Empowerment,'" said my colleague Bessie, who organized the workshop. Up until that moment, I had never yet heard the word "empowerment," but when Bessie says something like that, I take it seriously. So I went. It was the spring of 1988. The leaders of the workshop were David and Gail (see reference list at the end of this book). They made the case that we create our own reality. Everything that there is in our lives, is there because we have brought it there or allowed it to be there. The "decisions" about this may have been made much earlier, at a time that we no longer can remember (perhaps even in a previous life?). These "decisions" are of course by no means always conscious decisions. But still, our current reality is the result of our own creation process—still according to David and Gail.

The danger of a theory like this is that you tend to oversimplify it. That you confuse "responsibility for your own reality" with "having everything under control." That you apply an old Calvinistic morality whenever something unpleasant happens to you: it is your own fault. That you forget that our creation process is a process of co-creation with the forces of the universe. But I do like the theory, freed from all of these mistaken understandings. I had earlier applied it in my life, and I decided to apply it again.

Now at that time, I had a large debt. I had built it up a number of years before through a less than responsible spending policy (not keeping enough in reserve for taxes!), and also through taking great risks in my career. A number of times,

I chose for what I believed to be my integrity over my position. And I had also let myself be defrauded for a total of f40,000. With all this together, I had at that time a debt of f160,000, without even considering my mortgage (but this was balanced by the value of the house. At that time that was over $80,000. And more worth than now!). That is a lot for an independent practitioner. The income from my practice was in that year the same f160,000, which is approximately equivalent to a salary of f100,000 for someone in a salaried position. Quite a lot, but for someone with three children in school, living in a steeply mortgaged house, with a wife who had, at that time, no income to speak of, and carrying interest of f10,000 per year, still not enough to pay your debt off quickly (to pay off a debt of f160,000 you in practice need to earn a gross of double that). For years I had hardly bothered myself with this: I carried the debt with me from year to year. We lived well from it, and alas, the interest was tax-deductible.

But at that time I had suddenly had enough of it. The debt in fact hampered my freedom of movement. It limited the risks that I could take, and the investment in time and money that I was able to make. Suddenly after all those years, the debt felt like a weight on my shoulders. In short, I wanted to get rid of my debt.

In the workshop, we got the assignment to formulate what we really wanted. It must be formulated in the positive, for example not "no debt" but instead "money in the bank." My statement came out in another way, as follows: Next year, I want to have an income of f309,000 from my practice. A very high sum, practically twice the old income from my practice, and not possible for me to earn just by myself.

Don't ask where this wish came from. I could of course have said that I wanted a positive balance in all my bank accounts. Or that I wanted to own f100,000 free and clear. Or that I wanted to win the lottery. But I didn't say any of those things.

Probably I didn't trust any of those possibilities enough, or they lay intuitively too far off in time. "Too much scepticism doesn't promote trust in the theory or in its effect," said David and Gail, and I knew that, too. But in any case my wish was not the result of a rational consideration (other than that I wanted to get rid of the debt, and that earning more could be a good step on the way). It was a clear case of intuition, specifically the formulation of the wish. Where does such intuition come from? I don't know, but it feels like something that comes from outside (My angel? See before).

David made me stand in front of the group to motivate and express my wish. I did not find that easy. I had to conquer something to do that. This was a group of colleagues, and a number of them were direct competitors of mine. But perhaps it was more irrational, and I thought that I shouldn't talk about money in that way. Afraid of seeming greedy or something. In any case, it was a good test to see how forceful my wish was, and how much "contra-energy" I gave the wish with these kinds of undermining thoughts. David also tested me in my faith in my wish. He said, "Is what you wish completely unreal, or can it, in your fantasy, *really* come about?"

"It is possible," I said, "even though I don't precisely know how. Maybe there will be some income on a percentage basis, or more people will work for me on a percentage basis."

"OK," he said. "You don't have to know precisely how, as long as you have trust in it." He had me tell a fantasy out loud where it appeared that the wish was already achieved (Such a statement is called an affirmation in the theory of "empowerment"). I said, "Wait a minute. If I make this statement, is it true that I can't earn *more*? Aren't I also limiting myself through this statement?"

He laughed. "We have a trick for that, Why don't you simply add on the words 'at least'?"

"OK," I said. "I want to acquire at least f309,000 income in

1989." What a thrilling statement!

"And now the statement in which it appears that you have achieved what you wished, in the present tense," said David.

"I have made the income from my practice that I wanted to, and I am a satisfied person," I said, carefully avoiding the amount, so that I could potentially make even more.

"And now," said David, "you have to see a situation before you where it appears that you have reached what you truly wanted. For example, you tell it on your partner, or whatever. But see it before you, like a photograph, with as many details as possible." Immediately I saw myself standing by my desk and taking a bank statement out of an envelope. On the bank statement there was a positive balance of about f 25,000 (I have forgotten the precise amount) and I knew, furthermore, that I was not in the red anywhere else. A deep satisfaction filled me. I described this to the group. David wanted to test, in the group, how convincingly I came across, but he didn't have to do it, since I received a spontaneous round of applause.

And my income from my practice the following year? Three hundred and twelve thousand two hundred fifty-nine guilders and five cents. Through my own training and consulting work; through percentages from colleagues who worked with me; and through a small sum from authors' royalties. I swear to you I arrived at that the sum of f309,000 without rational calculation, or after making the income projection for the coming year. That was actually only done *after* this workshop, then twice revised upwardly until it was finally revised in August to f309,000 (to avoid misunderstanding, these sums of money refer to gross income: income before taxes, insurance and pension premiums, and salaries).

The Message From My Teacher:

This process is called "manifestation" by scientists, teachers, and consultants. That is taken to mean: to make things visible ("manifest") in reality which have previously only existed in your mind. The theory concerning manifestation says that we create or cause that to which we have paid conscious attention to or on which we have spent unconscious energy. Thus we create or cause what we want, what we desire, but also what we are afraid of, what we avoid, or what we suppress in ourselves. Attention and energy can thus be both positive or negative. In both cases they have their effect.

So the process of manifestation is continually taking place, whether we are aware of it or not. Because we also unconsciously give energy to things, and because our spirit often works paradoxically (we want conflicting things, or we desire that which we at the same time fear), the result of the manifestation—that is, our reality, our living situation—is frequently not what we want. There is also another reason that we often fail to have the process of manifestation under control: the elapsed time between giving energy or attention to something and the manifestation (of it) is unpredictable and can be long or short.

All in all, we must not confuse manifestation with having our lives under control. But it *is* true that the process of manifestation is an invitation to self-examination. Because the better we know what is going on in our minds, the greater the (level of) awareness with which we can choose where to give our energies (to), and the greater mastery we (are able to) acquire over our own lives.

II

At the end of that year, I can still remember well. I was reading the paper one Sunday, and my eyes fell on a small notice in the cultural supplement: "Turner Award." Turner Publications (the publishing department from the television station CNN) announced a competition. They were asking for a novel, taking place somewhere between 1992 and 2022, in which it must appear that things were going well with the world. Grand prize: a half million dollars, plus publication of the novel in book form with a first edition of 50,000 copies, and a possible film version, and all of this with the author to receive normal royalties. Both the second and third prizes would be published under the same conditions.

Now, I had always wanted to write a novel, and I found the assignment very seductive: I mean the nature of the assignment. Furthermore, the prize was not to be despised; just now the prospects for 1990 weren't that rosy, and now the plan for the school I wanted to set up was beginning to take form, but was provisionally held up due to a lack of funds. Also, even though my debt was indeed halved through the manifestation of my income from my practice, it was still f 80,000. But even more, a theme and the beginning of a plot flashed on me immediately. I also found it a remarkable coincidence that I, who never read the cultural supplement, paged through it this time and immediately saw that tiny little headline. *That couldn't be chance*, I thought. So I said to my girlfriend, "I have just now decided to earn $500,000 within one year, and I requested a registration form."

While I waited for the form, and considered when I wanted to write the novel (the coming summer, although we were supposed to organize a summer conference in England then), the plot played itself out in my head and began to take solid form. The characters in the novel began to stir themselves. They were like people in my own life, including me myself, but still they were different. The plot was good, but, unfortunately still incomplete, and therefore did not yet fulfill the assignment, even though I already had, in principal, an idea about what the message of the novel would be.

In the meantime I thought about the empowerment workshop from the previous year, and about the income that I had manifested. Couldn't I manifest the novel and the grand prize in the same manner? I realized that this was much more difficult, since my trust was much less. I also realized that if I were to apply the empowerment technique here, and it didn't work, it would take a formidable bite out of both my trust in myself and my trust in the manifestation process. In a follow-up workshop I brought the business up.

"Why don't you direct your energy to the school that you want to set up?" asked David.

"Because I want to do the one *and* the other," I said. It was clear that David intuitively didn't support my choice. But I kept on, formulated what I wanted, and saw the awarding of the prizes in front of me. No lack of inner thrill!

Still, as the summer approached, I began to be resistant to writing. It was not my first book, and I knew how strenuous it can be to sit behind the computer day after day while your mind is operating at top speed. I saw myself sitting at my computer—at home or on vacation—day after day. I simply had no enthusiasm for it, but, well, the grand prize called, and in and of itself writing a novel did seem very pleasant, and it was something that I had always wanted to do. Suddenly I realized that of course I didn't have to sit at the computer; I could also do it the old-fashioned way with pen and paper, and later (let someone) type it in. *That* was it: suddenly my enthusiasm for it came back.

The summer conference in England fell through and I set myself to writing. I was with my girlfriend on vacation in Vlieland. I had a real fountain pen with me that I hadn't used for years. It was fantastic weather. In the morning I wrote, sometimes also in the afternoon, interspersed with swimming, hiking, or bicycling. It was an absolutely terrific time. It was delightful to see how the people in the novel came alive, and I appeared to be able to shape a reality that began to live more and more. I felt myself to be literally godlike: creator of my own universe. The only problem was that the practical writing (typing) fell behind my mind, so that I was continually walking around with unfinished situations in my head. The plot was clear until approximately halfway through the book, but the end was still not truly satisfying. But in the summer that didn't matter, because I didn't get that far. I had to finish it in the autumn, but I still had time for that. The submission date was January 1.

In the fall I finished the novel. That proceeded less organically than in the summer. I had to fit it in between my work, and the end was more crafted than inspired. Nevertheless, the result was such that I sent it. However, there was still one more incident before that. My daughter, who had typed the manuscript, believed that she recognized old family problems in the novel, and thought that publication could be extremely shocking, especially for my ex-wife. She was so upset about this, that she almost didn't dare to tell me about it. I myself saw certainly autobiographical elements in the novel, but I had drastically altered the reality in the novel on purpose to take a direction that was more satisfying for me than the actual reality. But I did realize that the reading public, specifically those people who had a surface acquaintance with my wife and me, might think that I was telling the true story. I let one friend and one colleague read the manuscript; both of these, like my girlfriend, were interested, but not really moved. After all this you can feel the end coming: I didn't win any prize. This was a disappointment, but not truly unexpected. Looking back in retrospect, there were only a few periods when my energy was truly focused on manifesting the desired result, without undermining thoughts. That was immediately after reading the notice in the paper, and also during the writing in Vlieland. At all other times there was too much doubt; on account of this I let myself be influenced by counter-forces from outside, and my energy was too scattered. If I had truly taken a deep inner decision to manifest this-novel-with-this-content-coupled-with-this-prize, my behavior would have been rather different. In that case I would have spent much more time and struggled more deeply with it, just as long as it took for *me* to think that the text was 100% right. Even had I not then won the prize, I would certainly have offered the novel to a publisher. The fact that I didn't do that says enough to me. But the story is not yet finished, and neither is the novel! "What the future may bring..." I don't exclude the possibility that I could sometime take up this novel and its theme again. There are certain parts in it that I do think are 100% right. But as the Preacher once said, "For everything there is a season and a time for every matter under heaven" (*Ecc.3: 1*).

III

When I was still a psychotherapist, I belonged to a group, the International Saturday Group—a group that evolved from a therapy group in New York that came together on Saturdays—that organized yearly summer conferences under the leadership of Nadine, then my therapist and mentor. Hundreds of adults and children came together, from many countries, but the majority from the Netherlands, England, and America (the places Nadine worked): therapists, their clients, single people, couples, families. In two weeks a therapeutic community came into being, where unusually hard work was done, and where there was also a great deal of pleasure. People laughed and cried; screamed and sang; did theater and drew; made music and celebrated and did sports; and what have you. They were impressive and stimulating happenings that contributed greatly to the growth process of the participants, and for many became a turning point in their lives.

Still, these groups weren't for everyone. They dug very deep and they could be threatening for someone who was not ready for it. Formally, anyone could participate in this group, but in practice it was only the therapists in and around the Saturday Group and their clients and family members who joined.

Later, when I had left the Saturday Group, and also the profession of therapist, I began to wonder whether we could also organize something like that for people who were not in therapy: managers, professionals, people from organizations and their partners (I don't mean to say that these could not be in therapy!). There is a crying need for learning situations where really deep learning and growth can take place. In my experience, there exists a great hunger for emotional and spiritual development, for meaning, for a renewed perspective on life. In addition there was the fact that more and more managers came to me after a successful workshop and said that they wished that there was also something like this for their partner.

Now you are of course thinking: so why don't you go ahead and organize something like that? But it isn't so easy to organize something like that. Organizing that kind of conference costs a great deal of time and energy (and time is always money in my profession as organizational consultant). Furthermore, it is far from simple to lead such a conference (in the Saturday Group I didn't have the ultimate responsibility) and to form a good staff. And still further, a (crying) need is still something else than economic demand. I am convinced that there is a need for summer conferences like this, but would people who are not in therapy be willing to spend two weeks and a whole lot of money on it? Would their organizations reimburse them? And would they make the time available to their staff? Or would the conference need to come out of their vacation time? In the final analysis, it was not going to be a prestigious summer course from a business school or the like. Would the partners come? How much financial risk should we take? Questions, questions, questions.

I just began. First alone, on a small scale in the Netherlands. Two years later, together with a few others, for the first time on an international scale, in Switzerland. And when you begin that kind of project, where you put money in—we were among four colleagues guarantors of the costs: mailing, conference center, office costs—it is of the greatest importance that you listen to the feedback that life gives you, and that lets you know whether you are in harmony with the universe (in the language of everyday: if you have the wind at your back. Whether the time is right). By this I mean information which can come to you in many different forms. For example, in the form of feelings: do you have a lot of doubts or, in contrast, trust; do you have pleasure in it or is it burdensome? Or in the form of events: do the sponsor moneys come easily? Does the composition of the program flow naturally or is it really difficult? Can you easily get the speakers and work-group leaders that you want? Do the meetings of the organizing team go smoothly?

For Switzerland, the feedback was favorable. We knew precisely who we wanted to invite for lectures and workshops. And everyone we asked could and wanted to come at the time that we wanted, which can only be considered a miracle, given the complex international schedules (we are speaking about the top people in their fields on an international level, and it was already the spring before the relevant summer). The most striking example was Peter Goldman, an internationally known work group leader, whom we really wanted to invite to give a lecture and a workshop. I called him up, and said, "Peter, we would very much like to have you in the summer workshop."

"When is it?" I gave the date. "But I can't at that time; I have to give a workshop in Switzerland."

"But our conference is also in Switzerland," I said.

"Yeah, but I still can't come, except on Tuesday. I am free that day."

"But that is precisely the day that we had planned you into our conference."

"Well, then I do have to come." Peter is not insensitive to what Jung called synchronicity: the coming together of seemingly chance events.

The conference in Switzerland was certainly a success, but it brought us not a single cent. We would have been glad to have more people. We also couldn't pay the leaders as much as we had wanted to. We also made a number of small mistakes. But the feedback was very good. It was as if life was encouraging us, but at the same time warning us to remain modest. But we didn't listen to that. *We are going to go on*, we thought, and we made a plan for the conference in England the next summer. But there everything progressed with much more difficulty. In April we gave up: the registration wasn't going. ƒ20,000 damages, ƒ5,000 per person. How could that happen?

It appeared that our team hadn't truly functioned as a unit. Our energy was not fully directed towards the project: my energy was, for example, also on writing the novel. Two members stepped out of the team. My colleague Marga and I were left. It was June. Go ahead in 1991? It actually was not possible. We went into meditation. And then we knew when we came out: we are going forward, it is impossible, but we are going forward. And we also knew that the conference must take place in the former Czechoslovakia. Everything that happened after that is unbelievable.

To begin, I was phoned a few days later, by colleagues who asked me to give a course in Czechoslovakia. That made it possible for me to go to Czechoslovakia and to make contact with an organization that could help us to find a conference centrum. I went to Czechoslovakia together with my son. He had been there once before the velvet revolution. We followed our noses to the Rolling Stones Concert: the concert that was postponed in 1968 because the tanks, not the Stones, were then rolling. At that time Keith Richards had said, "We are coming back when the tanks are gone, and then we are doing it for free." That was now, seamlessly following the farewell tour of the Rolling Stones. I am certainly no Rolling Stones fan, but this was unforgettable. I think that the freedom celebration of that evening is only to compare with the celebrations after the velvet revolution and the fall of the Berlin Wall, with our own liberation after World War II, with Woodstock.

It appeared not to be so easy to find a conference center. Our colleagues in Prague had found three. One dropped out immediately: it was a horrible-feeling school building, where the spirit of communism still hung like a fog. We were shown around by the degraded business leader—the former Director—a sour apparatchik. Another center was a Kurort: nice, but really too large and too expensive for us. But the third...

When I saw it I was immediately sold. An old castle, fantastically situated. The comfort was not what I would have wished, but it was *so* beautiful...The atmosphere was very friendly, the staff extremely hospitable. The next day we heard that we couldn't have it, for really unclear reasons, typical of an East Block country in transition—I will spare you the details. "Keep trying," I said. "We absolutely must have that castle." And that also came about.

The brochure was gorgeous and commanded real attention (in one way or another the brochure for the English conference had become expensive and "fancy," and had very little impact). Finding the staff was no problem. Everyone that we asked wanted to and could come. We called Gail in America, and asked if she wanted to participate again. "Of course," she said. "I had already more or less reserved those dates in my calendar." And we hadn't even given her the precise dates before! But it did fit.

It was also Gail that brought us into contact with Omega: a large American training organization. Their staff were enthusiastic and served as co-coordinator. This brought the Americans to the conference. Gail was a source of enormous support to us; she became a true member of our team.

And then the conference itself. Everyone was on time for the opening, which in and of itself can be called a miracle. We started with gorgeous weather. But on the third day, when we had planned that the conference should focus on cleaning out of the old repressed pain, the weather was dark and gloomy. It rained, both out of doors and on the cheeks of the participants.

When we were dealing with the aggressive and destructive energy, which had caused problems for so many of us, and which now also sat within us, and which we wanted to recycle into a more positive force, people at a neighboring military base began to practice with fighter jets. I will never forget how one of the women, in tears, said, "I loved my father, and he loved me. But when my sexual energy developed, he dropped me from one day to the next." Vrooommmmmm....! The warplanes thundered over the castle. Similar coincidences occurred repeatedly. And when that day was over, and there was a party, and after that a day off, the sun broke through again!

It was a fantastic conference, where there was a great deal of healing, and where a base was laid for creativity and healing in the future. A network of friends throughout the whole world came into being, partially overlapping with the network from Switzerland. We made our share of mistakes here too, and there were still things to wish for. But the leaders and organizers could get paid. As Peter Goldman said, "Sometimes there are those moments that your actions are fully in concert with the universe and in harmony with the whole world."

IV

There were also four Hungarians in that same conference in Bechyne, who came from Budapest in a rattletrap car with hardly any money. After the first night Zsolt, the oldest, and the leader of that group, came to me with and gave me notice that his money and papers had been stolen from his car in front of the castle. With it was also the modest contribution that the four of them had been able to find for the conference.

This message created a certain panic in the conference group and everyone went to see if their car had also been broken into. Many people had left things in their cars, since it was a quite isolated part of Bohemia, and they didn't think that there would be auto thieves here, too. But not a single car had been broken into, neither the luxurious Western vehicles, nor the simpler, but easier to break into autos from Eastern Europe. Only our humble little auto from Budapest.

I had a conversation with Zsolt, bearing in mind, as I believe, that we create our own reality, and I asked him how he had set it up to let himself be robbed. He didn't understand this at all. He hadn't robbed himself; wasn't it actually the thief who had done that? Yes, but why then had he left his money and papers in the car? Wasn't that asking for trouble, I countered. Well, he had forgotten them in the excitement the previous evening. Furthermore, he had also been robbed the previous month in his hotel room, so that he thought that it wouldn't make much difference. My curiosity was now aroused: twice in one month, can you really call that chance? It appeared to be even less of a coincidence than I thought. He had been robbed six times in the previous year: at home, from his car, from his hotel room. "The times are like that now," he said. But that was of course nonsense: the level of criminality there is high in comparison with the old regime, but still no higher than in the West, and certainly not that summer. I pointed this out to him.

"Don't you see that you are really creating your own reality?" I continued.

"Yeah, but how?" he asked. "I am still not the one stealing from me."

"Well," I said, "in a certain sense you are. You can hardly call being robbed six times in one year a coincidence."

"Yes, but what is the role of the other, the thief?" he asked. "He also creates his own reality. So it must at least be the case that we are doing it together."

"Yes," I said, "but each of you is 100% responsible. If you didn't have a particular kind of energy and thought patterns, and attracted that sort of people, then it wouldn't happen to you. You indeed co-create your reality, but without your share there would have been no theft of your belongings."

"But what if he had suddenly decided to improve his life; then there would also not have been any theft," he said. "Then the theft would also not have taken place. So I am at a maximum only half responsible!"

"Maybe the theft wouldn't have taken place at that time," I said. "But unless you were to change your way of thinking, you would in any case be likely to attract someone else who would steal from you, perhaps even at that precise moment. The point is that you create your own reality, despite the fact that that may only become clear at a later time. Apparently you are trying, in cooperation with life, to tell yourself something, but you are poor at listening, since otherwise you wouldn't create the same situation over and over again, that you say that you don't want. What might the message be?"

But he was not ready for that. I, myself, am convinced that it was his negative, skeptical, and cynical attitude towards his fellow citizens that created this situation, while at the same time he desired to give up this attitude. In this way he created a crisis for himself that over time will force him to make a choice about how he will live his life (crisis comes from the Greek *krino*, to choose). He was at that time not completely ready, so that you wonder what he must create for himself before he can truly face his own thought patterns. I hope that it did not turn out to be a terrible crisis for him.

As things were, it was certainly an educational experience for the conference as a whole. It gave me the opportunity—in a large group—to go into how you can react to similar events: becoming defensive-aggressive; being perpetually on guard and blaming the hostile outside world; over time building up a suspicious or paranoid attitude; or taking responsibility onto yourself, while maintaining a realistic view of the world around you and staying open for what moves you and others.

His fellow travelers, in the meantime, were right there with us, and did take responsibility. One by one they came by to offer the maximum that they could out of their very scarce pocket change as their contribution for the conference. They had to give up their participation in the excursion in order to do that. I accepted their contribution to the conference as a generous action—it also moved me—but at another moment I proposed to the staff that they could go on the excursion for free. And so was it decided.

I have now lived in Amsterdam for a number of years. My car has never been broken into and my bike has never been stolen—until yesterday. The lock was very stiff, and could hardly open or close, and I took the lock upstairs for a minute to give it a lick of oil. One minute later I was downstairs again and my bike was gone. I even saw the thief riding away on my—no, in the meantime his—bike, but I was powerless. I, of course, also did this myself; probably I could have managed to close the lock, and I could certainly have gone and fetched the oilcan. And it might also not have happened. Therefore it is an interesting question: what did I want to tell myself with this? In my experience just asking this question produces much more—insight in yourself, strengthening of yourself—than is reached through remaining mad at another person who either really needed the bicycle, or who is also unconsciously unhappy with the life that he is leading. Would I like to change with him? At any rate I have a clear answer to this question: no. Were that otherwise, I would go and steal bikes.

V

Two years ago, in the fall, I was extraordinarily busy. I had a huge amount of work and was also involved with the development of a couple of new projects that lay especially close to my heart. I enjoyed all of it, and had also done it to myself, but it nevertheless began to weigh me down. It was like sitting down to a very rich dinner: each course is delicious, but one can also eat too much.

Now the most traditional manner to solve something like that is to give up certain activities. But I didn't want to do that. I didn't want to give up any paying work, since I was still busy paying off the last part of my debt. And as far as the unpaid activities were concerned, those were just the things that gave me the most pleasure and the greatest satisfaction.

Nevertheless, something had to be done. I began to get irritable and to sleep badly. I felt physically tired. And I had so much on my mind, that the quality of the various activities threatened to decline. I began to forget things and to make mistakes. And a number of the things that I particularly wanted—composing, singing, walking—I just didn't ever get to.

Now I believed, in the meantime, that I knew two things. One, that you create your own reality, and two, that time is not an objective physical quantity, a material unit like length or weight, but a subjectively created way of seeing the world. Not only Eastern mystics, but also Western philosophers like Kant and Bergson have said this. And actually this understanding also is a corollary of the theory of relativity and quantum mechanics. Therefore, I decided to use the methods from the empowerment workshop to create more time in my life. So, I pay attention to my desire for more time, and I make a statement which made it appear that I already have the time, and I imagine a situation where I could see that that had occurred (I have forgotten precisely which situation, but it undoubtedly must have been something like waking up on a Saturday morning and realizing that I had the whole weekend before me, and that there was nothing urgent that I needed to do. I could spend the whole weekend on my own needs!). I examine my undermining thoughts in relation to this process, and decide that they aren't a deciding factor. I repeat this procedure a number of times, and then leave it to life itself.

Nine months later I conclude that the problem is not solved. If possible, I am still busier, but this time it is worse. I am close to a breakdown. I lie repeatedly awake at night, and my irritation is now becoming obvious to everyone. In my work, a number of things are clearly going wrong, and the new things that I want to develop never get off the ground. My moods become gloomier. I analyze the situation. How can it be that I haven't manifested more time?

"You see, I think this empowerment method doesn't work at all. And time is an objective feature. You have a finite amount of it, and if it is gone, it is gone." Disappointed, I decide to return to the activities of the day, and once again consider which activities I will give up, as I suddenly realize something. I am doing almost twice as much in one week as a year ago. So I *have* gotten more time, but what have I done with it? Immediately filled the time with new activities, and thus created the same problem all over again, but at a different level.

I figure out that it wasn't at all that I want more time, but more rest, more rhythm. I was just deluding myself. *Enfin*, I correct myself, and go through the whole procedure all over again, this time desiring more rest. That appears to work: six months later I have too little work to supply my financial needs.

I panic, and I want more work, so in the coming fall I will probably be too busy again.

What does this teach me? In the first place that the business about "you create your own reality" is not a joke. We are truly enormously powerful, but we don't succeed in using our power in accordance with our goals. Apparently, this is something that we need to learn. In the second place it teaches me that I am still stuck in an old concept of time. I don't believe that I can have *both* enough rest and rhythm in my life *and* can earn enough. In my thinking, pressure and effectivity and rest are working as variables in a system that just will not come to balance. At still a deeper level—apparently I don't believe that life gives me what I need. And said another way—I believe more in scarcity than in abundance (of time and means).

There is a wonderful passage in the Bible, *Matth. 6:25-34*, from the Sermon on the Mount, that is very popular at wedding ceremonies and is immediately thereafter forgotten. "Do not be anxious about your life, what you shall eat or what you shall drink, nor about your body, what you shall put on...Consider the lilies of the field, how they grow; they neither toil nor spin; yet I tell you, even Solomon in all his glory was not arrayed like one of these...Therefore do not be anxious about tomorrow..."

Our heavenly Father knows about all of our material needs, and He shall take care of them, as He feeds the birds and the animals, so let us just concentrate on our spiritual development. Wise words, also completely in agreement with many other faiths: the Taoists, the Buddhists, the Stoics, to name only a few of the traditions. But can you *really* believe them? I have difficulty with it. No, that is actually wrong. I believe these words, but I am only a man of little faith, like Petrus and Thomas, and therefore I don't dare to fully act in accordance with these words. God gives you the nuts, but he won't crack them. For now I'll stick with the Preacher: "For everything there is a season and a time" (*Ecc. 3:1*), and, "Better is a handful of quietness than two hands full of toil and a striving after wind" (*Ecc. 4:6*). Just now when I typed in the "4" I hit the Caps Lock by accident. Guess what appeared? I'll let you see: $. If that is not a sign that life will take care of me, I don't know what is. Freud would undoubtedly explain it otherwise, but as the Preacher once said, "Much study is a weariness of the flesh" (*Ecc. 12:12*).

The Message From My Teacher:

All of the stories in this chapter are concerned with manifestation: making visible in the world of matter and forms what, until then, is hidden. It has to do with successes and failures. What we can learn from it is that we co-create the events and situations in our lives. But that doesn't mean that we always achieve success. Even when we consciously invoke the manifestation process—like in each of the stories, above, with the exception of number IV—we can either succeed or fail. Being aware of manifestation is a gradual learning process. For most people, it is only after a long time that it leads to greater effectiveness.

Why exactly is it so difficult to create what we want? In the first place because our minds are so complex. That can be seen very clearly in the second and fourth story. All of the limiting thoughts and misinterpretations can interfere with the achievement of the desired result. Because as I said, manifestation works both positively and negatively, and limiting thoughts and misinterpretations have just as much influence on what we manifest as our wishes and desires.

In the second place, it is sometimes difficult to create what we want, because our (process of) creation is always co-creation. We always create together with others, with nature, with life, with God. And we cannot control these. However, the paradox is that we nevertheless create our own living situation. One of the best illustrations thereof and of the traps we can fall into when dealing with manifestation comes in the next story.

Good Fortune Waiting to Happen

We—the publisher and I—have spent a long time thinking about the title of this book. We wanted to have a title that covered the contents well on the one hand, but was not too serious on the other. So we came to the title: Good Fortune Waiting to Happen. That this did not become the title was in part due to the fact that that title had already been used for another book. But I would still like to tell you what happened with the manuscript for this book, when it still had that title.

When the first version of the book is ready, it goes to the publisher. There, it is read in great detail not only by the editor but also by the publisher, and then the author gets it back with spelling corrections and suggestions for style improvements, all in writing. The sharpest critique came from the publisher, and concerned the commentary above, that consisted in the original version of two pages. As a result of her criticism I rewrote it completely. This produced a new piece of about one and a half pages. I also made significant changes elsewhere in the book. All in all it was still a quite a bit of work to make the book ready for printing.

I had promised to submit the book before my vacation (and business trip). I still had rather a lot of appointments that last week before the vacation, so that I hoped to have the book ready the week before that. I succeeded. Friday afternoon at 3:00 I typed in the last period and pressed the "save" button on the computer, after which I wanted to close the document. (This story becomes a little bit technical here. Keep reading, it gets clearer later on). Unfortunately the computer crashed just then, and I had no other choice than to turn it off. After restart, however, the document still appeared to be present, and before I did anything else, I also updated the backup. However, I made the mistake of overwriting the previous back-up, so that that one (the previous one) disappeared (There was only one back-up of the original version). After that, when I wanted to open the document to print it, that appeared to be no longer possible. The backup wouldn't open either.

To make a long story short, after extensive telephone conversations with experts, after many attempts to rescue the document with all different sorts of software and a trip to the Hague, it appeared that the document was definitely crashed. It was still there, but it was completely unreadable. All the work and all the creativity of the previous weeks had been lost. Tough luck.

I write all this now so matter-of-factly, but I can assure you that I was not happy, and that is an understatement. What should I do? Spend the last week before my vacation under enormous time pressure and redo all of the corrections and try and rewrite all of the altered passages? Or miss the deadline and start all over again after the vacation? Ultimately I did the first, but in the meantime I spent some time considering an important question: what am I actually trying to make clear to myself with this event?

I posed this question during the "Transformation Game" that I played that last week before the vacation with colleagues. The result of it is presented in the message from my teacher, below.

The Message From My Teacher:

Let us take a look at the original title of this book, the title of the manuscript and still the title of this chapter. What makes this title so nice? (Actually the dutch title was even nicer. The title—Happiness (or Fortune) lies in a small corner—is the opposite of a saying "An accident lies in a small corner," meaning that it can always happen, often most unexpectedly. In dutch the word accident—ongeluk—is the opposite word of happiness or fortune—geluk.) That it urges you to look at life and at yourself in a way that can lead to good fortune, but that it at the same time reminds you of a saying, "an accident waiting to happen," that precisely represents another world view: a world view where you don't have your life in your own hands, and where unpredictable and coincidental events can create a great deal of discomfort. The computer crash discussed above is an example of this kind of event. The proposed title and the saying also differ in another way. The title represents an optimistic view of life, and the saying a pessimistic one.

The process of manifestation described in the previous chapter means that we create situations of events to which we give our attention. We can see the world optimistically or pessimistically, and the world will, in practice, prove us. (Of course we cannot make ourselves believe that we see the world optimistically, if we don't believe it in our hearts. That sort of oversimplified positive thinking doesn't work).

Let's look again at the title of this chapter and of the manuscript. If we give attention to this title—and we did that when we thought up the title and made a decision about it—then we were giving attention to an optimistic view of life, that we then manifested. But at the same time, because of the association with the saying, we also gave our attention to the pessimistic world view, which we also manifested. Well OK, I knew that: an accident waiting to happen...

It teaches us how difficult it is in practice to always create the desired situation, and how our minds work in a subtle and, therefore, confusing manner. How can we create a situation in practice where our minds work more *for* us than *against* us?

You already know my answer: self-examination. If we learn how our minds work, then we are able to steer them. We can give more attention to what we want, and less attention to what we don't want. We can examine what we really believe and what we want to believe.

In this example, if we truly believe that an accident is (always) waiting to happen, then that will also be confirmed in our lives (if we believe that we will fall and are also afraid of falling, then we are sure to fall, see the story "Skiing."). But if we don't (want to) believe that, then we give no attention to that thought. And if it nevertheless comes up, then we say to ourselves: yes, I know this habit of thought in myself, but I would rather believe that what is waiting to happen is happiness. Thoughts are free, and we can choose what we think, as long as we are at least willing to let our old conditioning go. Seen in this way, life gives us a universe of possibilities and an unlimited freedom. It is like a spiritual trip to outer space. That is the reason for the new title of the book.

The meaning of the computer crash is thus the following: it stimulated me to think about the implications of the title of this book. Further, the crash forced me in particular to rewrite these and the previous pages (something which I without a doubt would NOT have done if only a small fraction of the text had been lost). Those just happened to be the pages about manifestation, and that is what it is all about. (It is also a remarkable coincidence that I was precisely working on those pages after the Transformation Game mentioned above; it thus took place just at the right time for me.) My point is that the events have deepened my insight into the manifestation process and have enhanced both the quality and subtlety of my exposition of manifestation.

Did I create the crash, then? Well, I believe that the debacle in any case would not have occurred without my share. If you read this story closely, you can also see that it consists of interactions between an apparently anonymous technical disturbance, and my reaction to it. Buy the way: that is a hallmark of all industrial accidents. An accident with an exclusively technical cause is just about impossible.

Manifestation is always a matter of co-creation. We create in interaction with the environment, just like we sail in cooperation with the wind, and grow a lawn in cooperation with nature. When I say that we create our own life situation, I am not saying that there is no such thing as circumstances which jointly influence the situation. The circumstances frequently determine the favorable moments for action, and the right time for doing something. You cannot make your lawn grow in October, and you cannot sail when there is no wind. But I do believe that there is no event or fact that occurs in our life, unless we have our share in (attracting) it. Therefore, each event and every fact has a meaning. Every event and every fact results from our actions and the flow of life in the moment. And the meaning always points on the one hand to towards ourselves, and on the other hand to the underlying forces of life itself.

Dark Night

Things began to go wrong in the spring of 1992. An old depression, an old rage which I thought that I had long before processed and was rid of, began to raise its ugly head once again. There were certainly triggers for it. For the first time in years, I had too little work, and thus too little income to satisfy all my obligations. I experienced a number of disappointments; people who didn't keep their promises, setbacks in implementing a number of new projects, and rejection of my manuscript from a publisher, after he had first accepted it. Society in general didn't contribute to being in a good mood either. Closer to home: the ways in which people acted towards themselves and others in the businesses where I was working were occasionally shocking. People were afraid, without being willing to face this. People were clinging to their positions and interests, both on a small and on a large scale.

And further afield: the world conference on Environment and Development in Rio became, completely in accordance with predictions, a demonstration of impotence. People in the former Yugoslavia were bashing each other's heads in. The violence in South Africa showed no signs of stopping. Half of Africa was dying of starvation. Saddam Hussein began to be restive again. It all made for a bitter disappointment after the hopeful years of 1989 and 1990.

And yet, that is not what it is all about. I have in fact been able to be happy during bleak times, and hope, faith, and love are not so much a function of the outside world, but come from within—or not, as now. Everything makes me enraged or grim. When I read about the destruction of the Dutch river landscape, and the way people are being treated there, I become so mad that I can't remain in my chair for long enough to read the story to its end. But I am just as enraged when someone swims into me in the swimming pool.

My girlfriend, who herself is also going through a difficult transition, can't stand it anymore, and we decide not to see each other for a little while. My relationship is in danger. Furthermore, I realize that if I can't manage in some way or other to get rid of this anger, I can just about forget my life goals. My life goal: that is to do something in and to give something of significant meaning to this world, specifically, a school for new leadership. If I go on like this, then I won't develop the capacity for it, irrespective of whether the talent is available in me. It seems dreadful to me to die without having the feeling that you have fulfilled your life. But still closer to home: my energy is already beginning to endanger my work. I am professional enough to limit my rage within my work, but the energy comes out indirectly, making me unpleasant to encounter and reducing my effectiveness. I am already going crazy from the feedback that I am getting about my work. "It was very useful, and so valuable, but...well...we had some difficulties with your directness, your confrontational style, your hardness..." fill in the blank. I can't let it deteriorate any further, otherwise I will lose the trust of my clients. Everything that I have built up, in business and in private life, and what I want to build, hangs in the balance.

How do I get rid of this, for God's sake? It is like a mental cancer. I thought that I was healed, but my mental cancer appears to have metastasized again. Apparently I didn't take the lesson of my bodily cancer sufficiently to heart. I don't have to blame myself for that, but now I am certainly plucking the bitter fruits.

I realize that my whole family is enraged, both from the father's and the mother's side. I have thus gotten my rage from no stranger, but also this knowledge doesn't help me to get anywhere. And this time I also don't want to give any energy on the causes from my childhood. I did all of that in my therapy: becoming aware, expressing, working through. It is more basic than that.

I decide provisionally to shut myself off from all personal contacts. No contact with friends and children. I am not in the mood, and I have no interest—as previously—to make them suffer from my destructive energy, or to play games with only half a heart. At best, the contacts with my friends and my children will distract me temporarily, which will only make the misery come back in a strengthened form. I cancel my singing lessons. I write my friend and colleague, Peter, and when his letter arrives, the affair has already become clearer to me.

In this state it is not sensible to wonder where the aggression, rage, and grimness come from. They are simply there, and they are forms of life energy. But they are far from usable, more likely to do damage to me and the world around me. Still, there are great examples of people who have used their rage very creatively: Krishnamurti, Jesus, Martin Luther King. You actually can't imagine them without their rage. They were also seldom joyful, at least, that rarely came out. Nevertheless, these are pre-eminently the people who inspire me. I don't want to compare myself to them, but let me at least be led by them in their direction. Then it thus becomes necessary to transform my own raging and depressive energies. And suddenly I clearly know what to do.

It involves making an inner decision; specifically, not to give any attention to this energy. When I become aware of this energy at a certain moment, I can perceive and recognize it, but after that I can continue with the order of the day. Not to repress it. Not to talk about it. Direct my attention willy or nilly towards something else. For example, if I become furious in traffic, I can listen to the music on my radio, or look at the landscape, or think of something pleasant. When a newspaper article makes me indignant, I can pay attention and ask myself, does my indignation come from love or fear or hate? In the last case I can direct my attention to good things that are happening in the world. If I am disappointed because of what people don't do, I can direct my attention to the things that give me hope and trust. And if none of that works, I can simply give as little attention as possible to my rage or indignation. But never suppress the rage or the gloom, since that strengthens them and the energy comes out in a veiled form.

I need to make a fundamental decision. Actually, I don't need to make it, I have to fall into it, like falling in love. I believe that that can only happen if I truly know that my life would otherwise be destroyed. That is already clear with my relationship: it is one minute before 12 and perhaps it is already too late.

I decide to consult the Transformation Game following the "Next-Step" procedure: drawing four cards that will refer me to what may be of importance for the next step in my life.

The first card I have to draw is a so-called group insight card: the insight that is important for my next step. On this card it says: *You have released your desire for personal gratification.* So I shouldn't be focused on personal reward or satisfaction. In other words, things only go well for me if I give up my craving, as Krishnamurti and Jesus and Buddha never tired of saying. It is a so-called group insight, so it is also of importance for the people around me.

The second card that I have to draw is a setback card, which tells me what is the most important obstacle in my way. That appears to be: *my dependence.* Dependence on what? Taken together with the insight, I think: on my craving, my satisfaction, my reward—on my need for approval, it said in the letter from Peter—but also on (my contact with) other people. On the one hand that makes me think in particular about my girlfriend, but on the other also on the opinions of gurus. And also about my dependence on what happens in the world. All this dependence is thus an obstacle in my way. I interpret that as follows: making contact with and being open to the world around me can make life richer, deeper, and more meaningful. But if I let the outside world determine my life I am not free anymore, and I am dependent. That led me to my dark night.

The next card that I have to draw is again an insight card and indicates how I can best overcome the obstacle. This card says the following: *Vulnerability is perfect protection. Being myself is safe.* I think it refers to my rage: part of my rage apparently has to do with defending—not being—myself, but building a wall around myself. But that creates false security. If I can let my defenses down, no longer need to defend anything, then I can't lose anymore and I create the safety of inner peace.

The last card that I have to draw is a so-called angel card. The angel that stands by me on my path is the angel of Harmony. I explain that as follows: harmony is within me, but I don't let it live. I could live more in harmony with life around me, in place of perpetually swimming upstream. I see three singing angels in the picture. Maybe I'd better take up my singing lessons again soon...

This period in my life strongly reminds me of the time that my marriage and my entire family life was in danger because I was spoiling everything, and we weren't yet at the point that it felt good to end the marriage. Then, too, it was 12 o'clock, and I didn't know if it perhaps wasn't already past 12. Then I also took a deep decision, and then, too, I was able to execute that (see the story "Crisis"). Apparently this is my life theme: something I have to learn in this life.

This renews my courage.

What the game made clear to me: this path is more than applying a clever technique. It involves radical change in attitude. On this path there is nothing against enjoying what life offers—eating well, contact with my children and my friends, going out, making love, pleasure in my work—but as long as I need these things in order to feel alright, I am dependent on them and then I begin to covet them. At that point I am no longer on the path I have to follow, and I lose my insight.

As I said: Peter wrote me a letter and sent me a tape where he orally discussed what I had written to him. Later I also spoke to him personally. He said that in fact I was at the point of going through an initiation process: "The stress of focus appears to move from the second chakra to the throat chakra which is the transformation of the reproductive energies into a higher level of self-expression."

A test to reach a new level of awareness. And the test is to keep believing in my own dreams and ideals. I am touched by his insight—that is exactly what is the issue for me—how can I keep believing in what I have to give and what I can give, "the higher level of self-expression."

He gives me advice to restore my lost contact with nature. Once again I have forgotten the importance of this (see the story "Miracles"). And beyond that, to value the fact that I am not alone, that I am a part of a group of non-physical beings who are wise, loving, and warm, but who don't give any specific advice. I am, as it were, one of their representatives here on Earth. "If you don't feel that," he says, "begin with a mental image, imagine it in front of you, and meditate on it. Over time you will feel it. Treat your project (the school for leadership) like a baby in a carriage. Enjoy it, take care of it, but you can't force its growth. And finally, look back at your life and see your path, how narrow it has been, and how you have continually taken the right route. A voyage of 1000 steps is not finished without the last step, and that is often the hardest."

Four months later.

It is unbelievable the things that can happen if you make

Room for Happiness

your way into and through a "dark night of the soul." Of course you have to do it by yourself—but indeed, you are not alone. It is remarkable what life gave to me from the moment that I faced my dark night. It is truly too much to list or write everything, but I shall still offer a selection. The first was that my girlfriend made contact with me again. I had planned to write her after my trip to America (see under), but she herself wanted to have contact again. Our conversation was deep, good, and loving, and the relationship developed further from that moment on. I began to learn what love without binding means—letting each other be truly free, taking nothing for granted, no attachment, no dependence, no patterns, no needing each other, more attention for giving than for taking—and miraculous perspectives and possibilities opened themselves to me.

In America I had to do a group, together with Joy, a colleague who had developed the Transformation Game and whom I respect highly. From the place of my dark night I considered myself unfit to do the group, and until I had fully faced my dark night, there happened also to be too few registrations. But from the moment that I *did* face it and considered not going to America, the registrations flowed in. As if the life spirit of someone from the group of non-physical beings that Peter had talked about had said to me: as soon as I see that you are facing your inner truth, I shall remind you that you have a task to fulfill in this world. For that matter, Joy said to me on the telephone, "Don't forget that you are not alone—hold contact with the spiritual group that is supporting you." Just as if she had heard Peter, which wasn't the case. Furthermore, the group in America was one of the best groups that I had ever done. The evaluation on the feedback forms was the highest possible.

In the fall I was in Findhorn at a conference on the topic, "The Power of Service." In Findhorn Eileen Caddy told us that she had just come out of a dark night. That flabbergasted me and supported me. When someone like her, so wise, with such abundant inner guidance, and someone who had brought so much into being (she was co-founder of the Findhorn community, a source of inspiration for thousands of people all over the world), nevertheless now and then must go through a dark night, who was I, then, to complain about it? She said, "Not everyone needs to go through depression and pain as part of their own growth process, but I apparently do."

Something else I learned in Findhorn was gratitude. I learned there to begin my morning meditation with counting my blessings. An outstanding antidote for the poison in the world.

It is now Christmas. I have spent Christmas eve and Christmas day alone (with the exception of a short visit to my mother), in relaxation and meditation. On Boxing Day, my girlfriend and her son have had dinner with me.

The world is in even more rotten shape than in the summer, and the economic forecasts are grim. But I have work in abundance. Life seems to be taking care of me. I still constantly feel the gloom and doubt from within, but my inner peace is gradually increasing. My sister sends me *The Essene Book of Days,* a guide to meditation put together by Danaan Parry, my colleague in America. This book appeals greatly to me and it will serve as a guideline for my meditations in 1993. Miraculous, how things come together. When there are so many miraculous, loving, and beautiful things in the world, I cannot believe that humanity's ultimate destination is destruction. There will still be a great deal of suffering, but "Finally a clear, beautiful day will dawn..."

The Message from My Teacher:

When we are in the middle of a crisis it makes sense to break off those contacts which are not useful at that time. It is of course consoling when friends and family try to cheer you up, but it works like a band-aid and delays your ultimate working through of the crisis. Also, it doesn't take away the cause. It is also possible that our gloom can become infectious, and then everyone gets depressed. Then we are all even further from home. In a crisis, we have to ultimately do it alone. That doesn't detract from the fact that the presence of others can be experienced as support. But the perception that they are there is enough, and at the same time really crucial, just like the presence of Job's friends among the ashes "seven days and seven nights." As long as they were silent it was good, but when they began to speak, it was out of the frying pan and into the fire.

However, it may become important to call upon mentors and therapists. Not that they have the answers, but they can help us find the answers ourselves. Many people go to consultants, therapists, helping professionals, astrologers, healers, or to workshops to find answers to their questions and solutions to their problems (the "Doctor, do you have a pill?" attitude). But it doesn't work like that. A good help-giver doesn't provide any solutions either, and a good oracle (like the Transformation Game) doesn't give any answers. It is our assignment to hoe our own row, and *the* way to do that is to look towards ourselves: who am I, what do I do, what am I going towards, and what am I doing? Then the answers come by themselves. "Know yourself," it said on the arch above the oracle in Delphi in ancient Greece. And that was a wise piece of advice.

In the story above, Peter Goldman was my teacher and therapist. He talks about chakras, energy centers in the body, each of which makes a connection with certain organs and certain aspects of our being. It is a natural process that the development of the chakras follows the progression of our life. But apart from that, chakras can also become blocked. A crisis comes about when the chakras don't develop smoothly, but with shocks and bumps, on account of the blockages.

In our lives, each time that a new chakra develops we begin a new phase. Sometimes life tests us. Are we really ready for a new phase? That is what Peter meant when he talked about the initiation process. For me, the importance of his comments was that I could see what was going on, and that had a calming effect on me. That is precisely how professionals can be useful.

Peter also referred to the group of non-physical beings which would support me. He already said that I was skeptical about this; that is why he advised me just to imagine them. I can't say that I have directly experienced this group. But if those on the cutting edge, like Peter and Joy (from America) take the existence of this group for granted and accept it, who am I to deny that they exist? I myself often have the intuitive feeling that we are guided (see, for example, the story "The Diving Board"). And that concept gave me courage during the dark night. It was good that Peter reminded me of this.

Earlier we went into the meaning of a crisis a bit. The word comes from the Greek *krino*, to choose. In Latin, crisis means a turning point. The Chinese, too, see crisis in this way: the character for crisis consists of the combination of two Chinese characters, which by themselves mean "danger" and "chance." So a crisis is the chance to choose anew, and so can become a turning point in our lives. From the foregoing it won't surprise you that I believe that that is precisely why we, ourselves, create crises. We create the opportunity to reorient ourselves in our lives, and to learn something substantially new. It is of course possible to learn without a crisis (there are also some examples in this book), but as a rule we are such poor students that we need a problematic situation for our growth process.

Room for Happiness

Therefore, what goes on in a crisis is finding answers to basic questions like, why and how do I do that? What am I trying to tell myself? What do I actually want to achieve? So it is about taking respons-ablility for our lives. We see in this book that merely finding the answers *once* is often insufficient. In a new phase of our life we frequently need to rediscover the answers over and over again.

When we face a crisis and don't run away from it, we often go through a period of great creativity immediately after that. That's why my group in America went so well.

The Good Shepherd
A Christmas Story

For Aletta

I heard the next story somewhere—but I no longer know from whom. I have filled it out and expanded it.

It is a silent winter night. There is no wind, and a deep calm has come over the earth. The shepherds who are in the fields notice how peaceful it is. The stars shine from a clear heaven. No sound disturbs the silence. The soft hissing of the fire is the only sound.

Suddenly there appears a clear light in the sky. Like a firework, but soft and calm. From within this light a figure comes down, and as it comes close to them the shepherds see that is an angel. And from this angel comes a voice, neither soft nor loud, neither male nor female—that tells of a miracle that they can witness in a manger nearby, and indeed invites them to go there. In the background is the sound of unimaginably beautiful music.

When this vision is past, and the shepherds, four in number, have recovered from their amazement, one says, "Come, let us simply go there and look." And so it is decided. But as they get ready to go, another considers that the herd cannot be left alone and unguarded just like that. What should they do? After some talking back and forth this last shepherd—who is a good man, who not only is very responsible, but generous to his friends—offers to remain watching the flock. The others thank him and take their leave.

It is a very long time before they come back. The shepherd who stayed behind encounters the deep silence of the night. It is indeed as if the world is holding its breath. The shepherd gets sleepy and gradually dozes. Just before dawn the others at last return, and when the one who stayed asks, "How was it?" the others can't give a clear answer. They talk vaguely of a mother and a child and a father, but they do not succeed in making it clear what was really so special about it. But it is clear that they are deeply impressed. They are deeply submerged in themselves, and the lines in their faces have softened. The shepherd who stayed behind can't get much out of them and shrugs his shoulders.

Time goes by, the years pass. With the years it appears that there is a certain distance that opens between the good shepherd who stayed behind and his friends. His friends sometimes talk about themselves and the world around them in an way that he can't really follow. Once he asks directly, "So just what is going on with you guys? I can hardly understand you at all anymore."

And they answer him, "Don't you remember that night, when we saw that light? You were there, right? Something happened to us, that time, right? Don't you remember anymore?" No, he doesn't remember anymore. And no matter how friendly he remains, and continues to care for his neighbors, and does his work responsibly, a vague feeling of uneasiness nevertheless begins to grow in him, a vague feeling of envy, that others have something that he doesn't have.

Thirty-three years later he dies. He doesn't yield to death easily, since he continues to feel, to the end, that his life is not completely fulfilled. His death struggle lasts three days. He doesn't give up. His wife and children sit lovingly by his deathbed, but his last feeling is pain and anxiety. On Easter morning he dies. They bear him with love to his grave, and he arrives in Heaven.

At the same time, Jesus arrives in Heaven. "Wonderful," says God. "I'm glad that you're here. I need you. That was not so easy down there but now it is finished. Good work. But now something else. I need your advice. I have here a shepherd, who understands nothing from the miracle of divine life, even though we put it under his nose. He was so occupied with his responsibility, and controlled his actions and thoughts so fully, that he didn't get it that it was a night of peace and the flock absolutely didn't need guarding. I actually don't know what to do with him, because he is truly the ultimately nice and responsible man, but he has unfortunately missed the essence of life. What should we do with him?"

"Yup, I know the problem," answered His Son. "Down below there I met thousands of people like that. It is not the easiest kind. Give me sinners or tax collectors, or people who are truly in misery: these are often easier to reach. The best thing seems to me to be that we give him a new chance. What would you think of a life as a priest? Or as a member of a contemplative order? Perhaps he will experience the mystery through prayer and ritual."

"Good idea," said God. And as it is said, it is done. The shepherd comes back to the earth, and—after growing up in a good Christian family, in the middle of the dark ages—he joins the order of Benedictines, for a life of pastoral work and prayer. He comes into contact with many needs of the people: poverty, sickness, fear, and doubt. He does what he can, always gives attention and time. But he lacks one thing: faith. He is able to imagine the divine mystery, but he doesn't succeed in experiencing it. And people feel that. "Pater Aloysius truly always does his best," say people to each other, "but he doesn't really understand you. He always stays so intellectual. You can't feel that he is in contact with God."

And in fact he isn't. As he gets older he becomes more desperate. "How can it be, in spite of everything, that I don't experience the divine mystery?" he wonders in despair in his cell, and also asks the Father Abbot.

"Pray and work, my son," the Abbot replies, "and God will surely have mercy on you."

Yes, if he only could be sure of it. Father Abbot could just as well have said, "Surrender, let yourself go, and try not to be so stiff." But, well, perhaps Father Abbot is also not so directly in contact with God.

After a devout and laborious life our shepherd/monk comes back to heaven. What now? Good advice is expensive. "Let him have some more suffering this time," said Jesus. "In the final analysis that didn't do Me any harm, did it?"

As it is said, so it is done. The shepherd gets a life of poverty, disease, and loss of loved ones. However, that is out of the frying pan and into the fire. He only becomes more resentful and rebellious. There are still more lives tried, easy and hard. As a musician, because music is also a way of experiencing God. But he focuses primarily on his career, and misses the message. As a woodsman, because God is present in Nature. But he becomes mired in management questions. As a rich and loved man, since material and spiritual riches sometimes lead to gratitude, and so to humility, and so to surrender to God. But he becomes fearful of losing everything, and holds on tight to his position. As a psychotherapist, since that could help him to have love for his clients and to see God in others. But he is by mistake born in the Netherlands, and develops extremely rigid attitudes towards good and evil, and because of this he never succeeds in unconditional acceptance of his clients. As a mother, so that he/she can experience God through pregnancy, birth, and motherhood. But he/she is afraid of the life force as it manifests itself in pregnancy, birth, and the child itself, so that he/she becomes overprotective of the child. As a prostitute, since Jesus had so much success with another one of those. But he/she only becomes hardened, turns into a heroin addict, and dies of AIDS.

And gradually, through all of these lives, an unconscious idea that he is missing the point about life began to fester in him. Others can find it, why not him? His despair grows and turns into desperation. From being aggrieved he becomes rancourous, rancor becomes resentment, and resentment becomes hate.

Finally God and His Son see no other possibility than to give him a life as psychopath and killer. "No matter what we do, in the end of course it stays his freedom and his responsibility," said God. "There ain't no predestination, and we don't play favorites here. We didn't arrange the fall from grace for nothing. He has the Knowledge, but the Redemption is still to come."

Down below, on Earth, it is Christmas night, and a lawyer is walking. The world is silent and peaceful. She thinks about her client, now sitting in prison. "Of course you can't approve of what he did, and it has brought about uncountable suffering," she thinks, "but nevertheless I love him. I know that deep inside him there is a good person, and by doing things this way he won't find happiness nor fulfill his destiny. Tomorrow I will go and see him." And with a shock she realized that if she could love *him*, she could love anyone.

"The ways of Humankind are inscrutable," God says to His Son, "but we are getting there. We only need to connect his spirit to hers, and his liberation is assured."

"Yes, but he still has to do that himself," replied His Son. "Although, she can do it, too. Then he only has to accept it. And there is indeed a good chance of that. She was one of the other shepherds, wasn't she—you know, his friends? As we once said, "Never be dismayed about goodbyes. A goodbye is necessary in order to meet again. And meeting again, in this or other lifetimes, is certain for those who are friends."

The Message from My Teacher:

This story is a metaphor that assists me in accepting the anger in myself, an issue with which I began this book (see "Cindy"). It has helped me better to understand myself and others; to judge them less, and to act with more compassion when I encounter them.

Epilogue

In this last chapter, I will lay out the essence of my vision of life. Now and then I will refer to the stories. You can also see this epilogue as a summary, and I shall therefore also feel free to repeat what I have earlier said.

The Flow of Life

I believe that life can be seen as a stream. Both my life and life in general. Comparable to a river which flows from the mountains to the sea. When we get to the end we are absorbed, but we don't disappear.

You can also see life as a process of universal creation. We are created in it, but we are also co-creators of it (that is my view of the symbolic meaning of *Genesis 1: 26*: we are created in God's image and likeness; that is to say, we too are creators). We can create in harmony with the greater process of creation, but also in rebellion against it, as in *Genesis 3*: eating forbidden fruit. That always creates problems and crises, but it also sharpens our awareness. In that example, we acquired the gift of discrimination and choice.

We are as if sailing on a lake. We create our own reality, but not separately from the forces around us. As sailors, we can determine where we make landfall, but not always how and when. In that, we are dependent on the winds and the waves. The wind and the waves always favor the best sailor. But to become the best sailor, we have to learn through our mistakes. For example, if we want to become an honest person, we first have to learn the distinction between honest and dishonest in our own experience. We shall occasionally have to do something dishonest and lie about it. Otherwise we can never choose to be honest—otherwise we are honest merely through conditioning.

Learning from Crisis

Many of my stories concern one or another type of crisis: "War and Peace," "The Diving Board," "Cancer," "Having Children," "Soccer," "Cindy," "In Memoriam Patris," and so forth. Looking back, there is no single one of these crises that I would have chosen to miss. I believe that I created them, piece by piece. Richard Bach says, "There is no such thing as a problem, without a gift for you in its hand. Men seek the problems, because they need the gifts" (*Illusions*; see reference list). And that is true. Each of the stories that I have told taught me something essential, which I was able to turn to my advantage, and on account of which I have been able to give something significant to my fellow humans (mostly in my work). Examples? Let us review the stories I have listed.

"War and Peace" taught me to build up my faith in myself and to have understanding for suffering and lack of faith in others.

"The Diving Board" taught me that I don't have to be stopped by my own fear, and also that fear is a natural thing. This experience taught me to understand fear when I encounter it in others. It was also the beginning of my belief in guardian angels.

"Cancer" taught me to have more care and love for myself, and to strengthen my own vitality. It posed basic choices for me about how I wanted to live, and taught me that creating my own reality is not a mechanical process, but an organic process of co-creation.

"Having Children" and "Soccer" taught me to make the

connection between the man in my father, the man in myself, and the man in my son.

"Cindy" taught me that cruelty and violence exist in me. It taught me to live with them without damaging others. It taught me that this is also present in others, and it made it possible for me not to react to these others destructively, and so to perpetuate the spiral of violence and grief.

"In Memoriam Patris" taught me that we humans in general (and I in particular) have to create our own hope. We can't sit around passively and wait until someone does it for us.

Manifestation

All of the experiences have taught me something about the "law of manifestation." In our material reality, what appears ("manifests") is that to which we have given our mental energy. It doesn't always happen immediately—sometimes much later. Thus our current reality can be the consequence of mental processes which took place much earlier, perhaps even before our birth. These processes can also occur unconsciously, but they will undoubtedly come to light.

Giving energy can mean: giving attention, repressing, avoiding, desiring, and still other things, consciously or unconsciously. In this process we can receive insight, through looking towards ourselves without judgement or approval or disapproval, and through taking the reality around us as feedback. With this I mean that we begin with a working hypothesis that the situation in which we find ourselves is always there because we have had a share in its coming into being. That can give us insight into how and why we are doing that.

In the above I have repeatedly used the expression "I have learned." But strictly speaking that is not quite right, since the learning process is continuing. The insight can first occur on the intellectual level, subject to many doubts. Later it becomes further anchored in my beliefs and my feelings. Learning in this sense is a process of developing, that is de-enveloping. Or discovery: the protective covers fall away. I come closer and closer to myself.

Self-Discovery

People naturally have a need for self-discovery. Just like a child will examine the world around him, just like a scholar will penetrate the secrets of his discipline, and just like the explorer will penetrate the blank spots on the map, so all of us want to penetrate the blank spaces in ourselves. But we are also afraid of the unknown. So there is always resistance and fear, which may be strengthened yet further through discouraging experiences in this and previous lives, or through pain and grief that we couldn't handle, and so suppressed ("War and Peace"). We too want safety and security, and we think—often unconsciously—that we can't handle the process of self-discovery. But when we stop on account of this we pay a great price: an unfulfilled life. And we *don't* have to let fear stop us ("The Diving Board").

Destiny

As a child, I was a member of the Socialist youth movement. When I turned 12, I had to move over to the "Falcons," and I had to promise to obey the Law of the Falcon:

*"We will strive towards the highest heights;
dig to the deepest depths;
and surround the world with friendship."*

Room for Happiness

A better expression of my highest goals in life I have actually never seen.

The purpose of life is to develop ourselves, and to be happy. Happiness is waiting to happen: there is always space for happiness and good fortune—it lies within everyone's reach. (How this could be true for people who live in miserable circumstances is another story—I certainly have ideas about this, but that's not for now). We are fortunate if we fulfill our lives, that is, living to the fullest, getting out of it what is in it, developing and using our talents to their fullest. That means that we do what we have to do, learn what we have to learn, and give what we have to give. You could also say it like this: live in accordance with our own destiny.

I do believe that there is something like destiny, and that we can find it through looking at the course that we have followed so far. My own course clearly has to do with building up hope and trust. Trust that life gives me what I need. Teaching me to surrender to life, in place of trying to make it happen, which actually doesn't work. The grass doesn't grow any faster when I pull on the blades, and as sailor I cannot command the wind or the waves. Nevertheless, surrender to life is not a passive process, because I am a creator. So for me it has to do with learning to create in harmony with everything that is—and learning from the moments when this doesn't happen, moments in which I create a crisis.

This process is not easy for me, and in fact is still continuing. "You teach best what you need to learn most," says Richard Bach, and this is also clearly another part of my destiny, teaching others what I still need to learn myself.

Credo

Here at the end of this book I am aware of how grateful I

am. Grateful for food, for warmth, for clothes and housing that are there every day. For the friendship and love that have come to me. For my health. For the talents and skills that I have received. For the trust that my clients place in me. For the care, the nobility, and the beauty that you can find in the world around you. And finally for my intuition, my "guidance," my teacher(s). I realize that it is good to stop and acknowledge all this. It makes me glad and contented, and that helps me to keep on growing still further, to bloom, and to bear fruit.

I would like to end with the works that more than anything gave me back my faith. It is a text that the minister Ter Linden read out as closing from the bible class that I followed around my fortieth year. I don't know where the text comes from.

I have a Jewish father, but I am not Jewish in the literal sense of the word, since Judaism is inherited through the mother, and also I am not circumcised. But I do still have Jewish roots; perhaps that is the reason this text appeals to me so much. But you will also see that the text harmonizes completely with what I have written here. As far as I am concerned, then, "Jew" in this text stands for someone who fights for their hope and stands up for their mission, a "warrior of the heart"; and "Israël" stands for the community of this kind of "Jews."

To My Grandson

It was asked of a certain Edmund Fleg why he was a Jew. He gave the answer in a letter to his yet unborn grandson.

People ask why I am a Jew. Well now, I will give the answer to you, my small, still unborn grandson.
I am a Jew, because the faith of Israel doesn't demand that I violate my intelligence.
I am a Jew, because in every time when despair cries out,

the Jew continues hoping.

I am a Jew, because the word of Israel is both the oldest and the newest.

I am a Jew, because for Israel the world is not yet perfect and humankind is trying to make the world perfect.

I am a Jew, because Israel places humankind and its unity above the different peoples and above Israel itself.

I am a Jew, because Israel places the Divine Unity above humankind, the image of God's Unity.

And I say to myself: from my forefather Abraham to my own father, our fathers have transmitted a truth that lived in their bodies, and now lives in me, and shall I not transmit this truth to those who are born out of me? Will you accept this from me, my child? Will you transmit it in your turn? Perhaps you will want to give that up. If that is the case, then let it be for a greater truth, if there is such a thing!

Works Consulted

A Course in Miracles; Arkana, Londen, 1985.

Bach, Richard: *Illusions, The Adventures of a Reluctant Messiah*; Pan Books, London, 1978.

Gershon, David and Gail Straub: *Empowerment, the Art of Creating Your Life as You Want It*; Dell, New York, 1989.

Gibran, Kahlil: *The Prophet*; Heinemann, London, 1926.

Siegel, B.S,: *Love, medicine and miracles. Lessons learned about self-healing from a surgeon's experience with exceptional patients*; Harper, New York, 1986

Simonton, O. Carl, Stephanie Matthews-Simonton en James L.

Creighton: *Getting Well Again*; Bantam, New York, 1978

Wilber, Ken: *Grace and Grit*; Shambala, Boston , 1991